Destinations 1
Writing for Academic Success

Nancy Herzfeld-Pipkin
GROSSMONT COLLEGE

THOMSON
HEINLE

Australia • Canada • Mexico • Singapore • Spain • United Kingdom • United States

THOMSON

HEINLE

Destinations 1: Writing for Academic Success
Nancy Herzfeld-Pipkin

Editorial Director: *Joe Dougherty*
Publisher: *Sherrise Roehr*
Acquisitions Editor, Academic ESL: *Tom Jefferies*
VP, Director of Content Development: *Anita Raducanu*
Director of Product Marketing: *Amy Mabley*
Director of Global Marketing: *Ian Martin*
Executive Marketing Manager: *Jim McDonough*
Senior Field Marketing Manager: *Donna Lee Kennedy*
Editorial Assistant: *Katherine Reilly*

Development Editor: *Sarah Barnicle*
Project Manager: *Tunde Dewey*
Senior Print Buyer: *Mary Beth Hennebury*
Compositor: *Parkwood Composition Service*
Cover Designer: *Gina Petti/Rotunda Design House*
Printer: *Globus Printing & Packaging*
Illustrations: *Scott MacNeill*
Cover Image: *© Getty Images/RubberBall Productions/RF*
Photo Researcher: *Erika Hokanson*

For more information contact Thomson Heinle, 25 Thomson Place, Boston, Massachusetts 02210 USA, or you can visit our Internet site at elt.heinle.com

For permission to use material from this text or product, submit a request online at http://www.thomsonrights.com

Any additional questions about permissions can be submitted by email to thomsonrights@thomson.com

ISBN-13: 978-1-4130-1935-3
ISBN-10: 1-4130-1935-8

(International Student Edition)
ISBN-13: 978-1-4130-2296-4
ISBN-10: 1-4130-2296-0

Library of Congress Control Number: 2007932078

Dedication

*T*o my students, who always provide new insight and understanding no matter how many years I have been teaching, and who continue to make my job a most rewarding one.

Acknowledgments

As always, I am extremely grateful to friends and family for their understanding and support. I especially want to thank my boys, Jack, Seth, and Scot, for always "being there" for me and my friend Jean Riley for always providing feedback for ideas about my books.

Thanks to my ESL colleagues at Grossmont College, Donna Tooker and Virginia Berger, who provided feedback during various stages of writing, and Sara Ferguson, who class tested these materials.

Several other people were helpful in brainstorming ideas and providing feedback and expertise on specific units.

Unit One: Tammy Huston (Grossmont College)
Unit Three: Danny Martinez (Grossmont College), Julio Cesar Martha Mitre
Unit Four: Nancy Davis (Grossmont College), Linda Snider (Grossmont College), Mark Presnell (Grossmont College), Jack Pipkin
Unit Five: Andrea Garzenelli (Grossmont College), Paula Emmert

Many thanks also go to the people at Heinle. In particular, I thank Sherrise Roehr and Sarah Barnicle for helping make this series a reality.

Contents

Unit One   The U.S. Learning Experience
            (Personal Development/Study Skills)

Part 1   Unit Preview   **2**
Preview Activity: Course Expectations/Classroom Behavior
    Questionnaire   2
Quickwrite/Freewrite   3

Part 2   Reading and Vocabulary   **3**
Reading: How to Be a Student in a U.S. Classroom   3
Comprehension Check   4
    A. Main Idea/Details   4
    B. Understanding Details   5
Vocabulary Study   5
Discussion/Writing   7

Part 3   Writing Sentences—Basic Sentence Patterns   **8**
Reading: Choosing and Scheduling Classes   8
Questions   8
Explanation: Basic Sentence Patterns   8
    (subject + verb; subject + verb + object)
    Practice: Sentence Patterns   11
    A. Identifying Sentence Parts   11
    B. Writing Sentences—Word Order   11
    C. Writing Your Own Sentences   11
    D. Finding Sentence Problems   12
Discussion/Writing   12

Part 4   Writing—Introduction to Paragraphs   **13**
Paragraph Format   13
Paragraph Discussion—Format   13
Practice: Titles   15
Practice: Paragraph Format   15
Paragraph Discussion—Organization   16
    Topic Sentences and Details   17
        Topic Sentences   17
        Topics and Controlling Ideas   18
        Practice: Topics and Controlling Ideas   18
        Writing Good Topic Sentences   19
        Practice: Topic Sentences   20
    Support: Providing Examples   21
        Paragraph Discussion—Using Examples for Support   22
        Practice: Supporting Paragraphs with Examples   23

A. Identifying Parts of a Paragraph   23
B. Matching: Topic Sentences and Examples   24
C. Examples to Fit Topic Sentences   24
Discussion/Writing   25
Writing Assignment   26
  Picking the Topic   26
  The Writing Process   26
Following the Steps in the Writing Process   27
  Before You Write   27
    Step One: Thinking about the Topic/Getting Ideas 27
    Step Two: Organizing Your Thoughts and Ideas   28
    Step Three: Getting Feedback about the Chart   28
  When You Write   28
    Step Four: Writing the First Draft (Rough Draft) 28
  After You Write   29
    Check Your Work (Checklist)   29
    Step Five: Getting Feedback about the First Draft 30
    Step Six: Making Changes   30
    Step Seven: The Final Draft   30
  Chart: Organizing Your Thoughts for Writing   31

Unit Two   Body Decoration and Culture (Cultural Anthropology)

Part 1   Unit Preview   **34**
Preview Activity: Discussion Questions and Body Decoration
Recognition   34
Quickwrite/Freewrite   34

Part 2   Reading and Vocabulary   **35**
Reading: Body Art and Decoration   35
Comprehension Check   36
  A. Main Ideas/Details   36
  B. Understanding Details   36
Vocabulary Study   37
Discussion/Writing   39

Part 3   Writing Sentences—More Sentence Patterns   **39**
Reading: Reasons for Body Art/Decoration   39
Questions   40
Explanation: More Sentence Patterns (linking verbs with
  adjectives/prepositions of place/nouns/*there* as subject)   40
Practice: Sentence Patterns—Using Linking Verbs and *There* as Subject 42
  A. Identifying Sentence Parts   42
  B. Matching   43
  C. Writing Sentences—Word Order   43
  D. Writing Your Own Sentences   44
  E. Finding Sentence Problems   44
Discussion/Writing   45

Part 4   Writing—Paragraphs Using Description   **45**
Reading: Henna and Bridal Celebrations   45
Paragraph Discussion   45
Paragraph Organization—Using Description   46
Practice: Description   46
    A. Finding Descriptive Words   46
    B. Recognizing Vivid Descriptions   47
    C. Writing Descriptive Sentences   48
Review: Titles and Topic Sentences   48
Practice: Topic Sentences and Supporting Sentences Using Description   48
    A. Identifying Topic Sentences and Supporting Details   48
    B. Identifying Topic Sentences and Descriptive Support   49
    C. Identifying Parts of a Descriptive Paragraph   51
Discussion/Writing   52
Writing Assignment   52
    Picking the Topic   52
    Practice with Description   53
Following the Steps in the Writing Process   53
    Before You Write   53
        Step One: Thinking about the Topic/Getting Ideas   53
        Step Two: Organizing Your Thoughts and Ideas   55
        Step Three: Getting Feedback about the Chart   55
    When You Write   55
        Step Four: Writing the First Draft (Rough Draft)   55
    After You Write   56
        Check Your Work (Checklist)   56
        Step Five: Getting Feedback about the First Draft   56
        Step Six: Making Changes   57
        Step Seven: The Final Draft   57
    Chart: Organizing Your Thoughts for Writing   58

Unit Three   Mexican Americans (History)

Part 1   Unit Preview   **60**
Preview Activity: Discussion Questions and Maps   60
Quickwrite/Freewrite   61

Part 2   Reading and Vocabulary   **62**
Reading: Early History of Mexican Americans   62
Comprehension Check   63
    A. Main Idea   63
    B. Details   63
Vocabulary Study   64
Discussion/Writing   66

**Part 3   Writing Sentences—Sentence Combining
            with Coordinating Conjunctions**   **66**

Reading: Migration North   66
Questions   67
Explanation: Combining Sentences with Coordinating Conjunctions
    (*and / but / so / or*)   67
    Practice: Sentence Combining—Using Coordinating Conjunctions   70
    A. Identifying Clauses and Coordinating Conjunctions   70
    B. Matching Clauses   70
    C. Combining Sentences   71
    D. Choosing the Correct Conjunction to Combine Sentences   71
    E. Completing Sentences on Your Own   72
    F. Finding Sentence Problems   73
        1. Run-ons   73
        2. Comma Splices   74
        3. Run-ons and Comma Splices   74
Discussion/Writing   75

Part 4   Writing Paragraphs—Facts/Biographies   **76**

Reading: The Bracero Program   76
Paragraph Discussion   76
Paragraph Organization
    Supporting Sentences/Using Facts   77
    Paragraph Organization Review   77
    Concluding Sentences   77
    Restating the Topic Sentence/Main Idea of the Paragraph   77
Practice: Paragraph Organization—Topic Sentences, Supporting
    Facts, and Conclusions   78
    A. Paragraph Analysis   78
    B. Paragraph Analysis   80
    C. Paragraph Organization   81
Biographies   82
Reading: Dolores Huerta   82
Paragraph Discussion—Biography   82
Practice: Paragraph Organization   83
    A. Paragraph Organization   83
    B. Writing a Conclusion   84
Discussion/Writing   84
Writing Assignment   85
    Picking the Topic   85
Following the Steps in the Writing Process   85
    Before You Write   85
        Step One: Thinking about the Topic/Getting Ideas   85
        Step Two: Organizing Your Thoughts and Ideas   86
        Step Three: Getting Feedback about the Chart   87
    When You Write   87
        Step Four: Writing the First Draft (Rough Draft)   87
    After You Write   87
        Check Your Work (Checklist)   87

Step Five: Getting Feedback about the First Draft   89
Step Six: Making Changes   89
Step Seven: The Final Draft   89
Chart: Organizing Your Thoughts for Writing   90

Unit Four   Jobs and the Workplace
(Business and Workplace English)   91

Part 1   Unit Preview   92
Preview Activity: Discussion and Office Equipment Identification   92
Quickwrite/Freewrite   92

Part 2   Reading and Vocabulary   92
Reading: The Changing Workplace   93
Comprehension Check   94
    A. Main Ideas   94
    B. Details   94
Vocabulary Study   95
Discussion/Writing   97

**Part 3   Writing Sentences—Making
Connections with Transitions   98**
Reading: Job Applications   98
Questions   98
Explanation: Using Introductory Transitions   99
    Practice: Using Introductory Transitions   101
    A. Identifying Introductory Transitions   101
    B. Matching Sentences with Logical Relationships   102
    C. Choosing the Transition—Meanings   102
    D. Filling in the Correct Transition   104
    E. Completing Sentences on Your Own   104
    F. Finding Sentence Problems   105
Discussion/Writing   105

**Part 4   Writing Paragraphs—Instructions/
Procedures/Chronology   106**
Reading: Job Interviews   106
Paragraph Discussion   106
Paragraph Organization: Using Chronology with
    Instructions/Procedures   107
Practice: Chronology with Instructions/Procedures   107
Paragraph Organization: Support for Procedures/Instructions
    and Concluding Sentences   108
Practice: Paragraph Organization—Topic Sentences, Chronological
    Support, and Concluding Sentences   109
    A. Identifying Support for Steps in a Procedure   109
    B. Identifying Parts of a Paragraph and Choosing a Conclusion   109
    C. Writing a Complete Paragraph   110

Discussion/Writing   113
Writing Assignment   113
   Picking the Topic   113
Following the Steps in the Writing Process   113
   Before You Write   113
      Step One: Thinking about the Topic/Getting Ideas   113
      Step Two: Organizing Your Thoughts and Ideas   114
      Step Three: Getting Feedback about the Chart   115
   When You Write   115
      Step Four: Writing the First Draft (Rough Draft)   115
   After You Write   116
      Check Your Work (Checklist)   116
      Step Five: Getting Feedback about the First Draft   117
      Step Six: Making Changes   117
      Step Seven: The Final Draft   117
   Chart: Organizing Your Thoughts for Writing   118

Unit Five   Technology and Education (Science and Technology)   119

Part 1   Unit Preview   **120**
Preview Activity: Questionnaire—Is Distance Education Right for You? 120
Quickwrite/Freewrite   121

Part 2   Reading and Vocabulary   **122**
Reading: Distance Education/Learning   122
Comprehension Check   123
   A. Main Ideas   123
   B. Details   123
Vocabulary Study   124
Discussion/Writing   126

Part 3   Writing Sentences—Sentence Combining with Subordinating Conjunctions   **126**
Reading: Technology in the Classroom   127
Questions   127
Explanation—Combining Sentences with Subordinating
   Conjunctions (*because* / *if*)   128
   Practice: Sentence Combining—Using Subordinating
      Conjunctions (*because* / *if*)   131
   A. Identifying Clauses and Subordinating Conjunctions 131
   B. Matching Clauses   132
   C. Combining Sentences   132
   D. Completing Sentences on Your Own   135
   E. Finding Sentence Problems   135
Discussion/Writing   138

Part 4   Writing Paragraphs—Opinions/Reasons   139
Reading: Distance Learning—An Excellent Educational Experience   139
Paragraph Discussion   139
Paragraph Organization: Supporting Sentences—Giving
    Opinions and Reasons   140
Practice: Identifying Facts and Opinions   141
Practice: Paragraph Organization   141
Discussion/Writing   143
Writing Assignment   143
    Picking the Topic   143
Following the Steps in the Writing Process   144
    Before You Write   144
        Step One: Thinking about the Topic/Getting Ideas   144
        Step Two: Organizing Your Thoughts and Ideas   145
        Step Three: Getting Feedback about the Chart   145
    When You Write   146
        Step Four: Writing the First Draft (Rough Draft)   146
    After You Write   146
        Check Your Work (Checklist)   146
        Step Five: Getting Feedback about the First Draft   147
        Step Six: Making Changes   147
        Step Seven: The Final Draft   147
    Chart: Organizing Your Thoughts for Writing   148

**Unit Six   Myths/Fables/Legends/Folk Stories
(Cross Cultural Stories/Literature)   149**

Part 1   Unit Preview   150
Preview Activity: What Stories Do You Know?   150
Quickwrite/Freewrite   150

Part 2   Reading and Vocabulary   151
Reading: Traditional Storytelling (i.e., flood or creation of humans)   151
Comprehension Check   152
    A. Main Ideas   152
    B. Details   152
Vocabulary Study   153
Discussion/Writing   155

**Part 3   Writing Sentences—Sentence Combining
with Subordinating Conjunctions of Time   155**
Reading: The Beginning of Earth and People   155
Questions   156
Explanation: Combining Sentences with Subordinating
    Conjunctions of Time (*before/after/when/while/as/until*)   156
    Practice: Sentence Combining—Using Subordinating
        Conjunctions of Time   159

A. Identifying Clauses and Conjunctions   159
B. Fill in the Blanks   159
C. Combining Sentences   160
D. Review of Coordinating and Subordinating Conjunctions   161
E. Completing Sentences on Your Own   162
F. Finding Sentence Problems   163
Discussion/Writing   166

**Part 4   Writing Paragraphs—Narration/
            Storytelling/Chronology   167**
Reading: How the World Burst from an Egg   167
Paragraph Discussion   167
Paragraph Organization—Narration and Chronology   168
Narration   168
Chronology Review   168
Practice: Paragraph Organization—Narration and Chronology   168
A. Words of Chronology   168
B. Paragraph Analysis   169
C. Chronology Exercise   170
Discussion/Writing   171
Writing Assignment   171
Picking the Topic   171
Following the Steps in the Writing Process   172
Before You Write   172
Step One: Thinking about the Topic/Getting Ideas   172
Step Two: Organizing Your Thoughts and Ideas   173
Step Three: Getting Feedback about the Chart   173
When You Write   173
Step Four: Writing the First Draft (Rough Draft)   173
After You Write   174
Check Your Work (Checklist)   174
Step Five: Getting Feedback about the First Draft   175
Step Six: Making Changes   175
Step Seven: The Final Draft   175
Chart: Organizing Your Thoughts for Writing   176

Appendix   177

From Paragraphs to Essays   178
   Review of Paragraphs   178
   Expanding Paragraphs into Essays   179
   Paragraph to Essay Discussion   180
   Practice: Expanding Paragraphs into Essays   183

Journal Writing   188

Timed Writing   189

Feedback: Peer Review   190

Sentence Writing Charts   207
   Basic Sentence Patterns   207
   Sentence Combining—
      Coordinating and Subordinating Conjunctions   208

Vocabulary Index   209

Skills Index   211

Preface

Destinations: Writing for Academic Success, Book 1 is designed to be used with high-beginning/low-intermediate level students of English. This text consists of six units, which have each been divided into four parts: preview, reading, sentence level writing, and paragraph writing. The main focus of *Destinations 1* is the writing of paragraphs through the writing process relating to specific academic and workplace themes. The text also covers vocabulary development, some reading skills, critical thinking through discussion and journal writing, and an introduction to essay writing in the Appendix.

The bulk of each unit is made up of exercises and activities that afford students as much active involvement as possible. Some of the readings have been adapted from other print sources. The themes of the units are academic or real-world in nature and are intended to introduce students to some of the ideas and content they will find in other (non-ESL) classes or in the workplace.

Finally, studying in a college or university environment can be a daunting task, especially for those students studying in the United States whose first language is not English. In addition to dealing with more obvious language problems, students from other cultures or countries may have difficulty succeeding in native speaker environments due to differences in both background and cultural information. This book is intended to fill some of those gaps in order to help prepare non-native speakers for the academic writing they will be expected to produce in courses throughout their college careers.

To *the* Teacher

Destinations: Writing for Academic Success, Book 1 presents and provides practice with academic writing based on specific academic or workplace themes and content introduced through readings. The book is divided into six units, each of which focuses on writing at the sentence level and the paragraph level. Each unit also presents some practice with reading skills (such as comprehension), vocabulary development, and critical thinking.

General Notes About Materials and Activities in This Book

In some sections, discussions or explanations are provided in the form of questions and answers. Teachers are encouraged to present this material in their own class discussions before reviewing these sections of a unit. Then these sections of the book can serve as review of the in-class discussions.

Each lesson includes a variety of activities and exercises. This will afford students many opportunities to participate, as well as offer students a chance to express themselves in varied ways using different language skills. Due to the variations in length and purpose of individual classes, it is not expected that every teacher will cover everything in each lesson. Teachers should feel free to choose those exercises and activities that best suit the needs and abilities of their particular students.

Working in pairs and groups is encouraged throughout this book. Many of the exercises and activities are well-suited for this kind of work; those that lend themselves particularly well to group or pair work have this icon next to them.

Following are more detailed descriptions of all the parts and suggestions on how to present or follow up on them.

Unit Organization

Part 1: Preview

Part 1 of each unit introduces the topic or theme of the lesson through either discussion or a short activity, such as looking at photographs or maps, or answering a questionnaire. The preview is meant to activate schemata for the students and to give the teacher an idea of what the students might already know about the topic. If students know very little about the topic, Part 1 will serve as an introduction. A quickwrite/freewrite is also included here to give the students a chance to write freely on a subject that is related to the content of the unit.

Part 2: Reading and Vocabulary

In Part 2, the main reading of the unit is presented. This is the longest reading of each unit and presents both the theme and related vocabulary. Teachers may want to discuss the content of this material before students complete the exercises that follow. In addition, it is recommended that readings be assigned as homework along with some of the exercises that follow (such as comprehension and vocabulary). The ideas and vocabulary items presented in this part are recycled in a number of ways:

- through discussion/writing topics that follow in the unit
- in exercises and activities in other parts of the unit
- in final writing assignments
- in the accompanying grammar workbook (*Destinations: Grammar for Academic Success, Book 1*)
- in word part and word form exercises on the student Website

Part 3: Writing Sentences

In Part 3, writing is presented and practiced at the sentence level in a systematic way through various sentence-pattern and some sentence-combining techniques and through work with sentence problems, such as fragments, run-ons, and comma splices.

In each unit, Part 3 begins with a short reading that includes examples of the sentence-patterns or sentence-combining techniques to be discussed and practiced. Students are then asked to analyze parts of the reading by answering several questions. This section provides an inductive exercise for students to figure out (or state as review) the grammar and mechanics of the particular sentence-pattern or sentence-combining technique. An explanation section immediately follows in order to ensure that students understand the topic fully. Following these explanations are exercises and activities that provide sentence writing practice.

- Sentence problems (fragments, run-ons, and comma splices)

In the explanation section, a discussion of related sentence problems is provided. For example, in the units that present the use of subordinating conjunctions with dependent clauses, part of the explanation discusses problems of fragments and run-ons related to incorrect use of these clauses. Furthermore, each unit includes exercises that provide practice in identifying and/or editing these problems.

Part 4: Writing Paragraphs

- Part 4 covers various aspects of organizing and writing paragraphs. Organizational patterns (examples, description, using facts and opinions, etc.) that students are likely to encounter in college classes are discussed in different units.
- At the end of each unit, students are given a choice of writing assignments related to the topic. These assignments will elicit as much of the information studied and practiced in the unit as possible regarding vocabulary, sentence writing, and organizational techniques.
- The writing process is explained in Unit One. After the final writing assignment in each unit is given, students are asked to follow the

steps in the process. These steps are tailored to the particular assignments given. Also provided in Part 4 are:

- some prewriting devices such as charts and outlines, for students to fill in before they write
- checklists that help students review their work before handing in their assignments.

Discussion/Writing Sections

Throughout each unit, questions for discussion and/or writing are provided. Teachers may utilize these questions in different ways:

- to stimulate thinking about and discussion of the information presented in the various parts of the unit.
- to provide students with an opportunity to write informally (journal writing, freewriting, etc.) before they are asked to write a more formal assignment at the end of the unit. Topics that are particularly suited for journal writing are indicated with this icon in the margin.
- to help students think about and prepare topics for the writing assignment at the end of the unit.

Appendix

The appendix includes the following sections:

- From Paragraphs to Essays
- Journal Writing—a short explanation of how best to use this type of writing
- Timed Writing—a short explanation about in-class timed writing as well as tips on how to budget time
- Feedback: Peer Review—a short explanation with two peer review sheets per unit for students to fill out: one for review of the organization chart and one for review of the first draft of the final writing assignment
- Sentence Pattern Chart—chart of sentence patterns discussed in Units One and Two.
- Sentence Combining Chart—chart of coordinating and subordinating conjunctions discussed in Units Three, Five, and Six.
- Vocabulary Index—an alphabetized list of all vocabulary presented in the units with page numbers where the words first occur.
- Skills Index—an alphabetized list of all skills taught in the book including writing, reading, and critical thinking skills.

MATERIALS AND ACTIVITIES ON THE WEB:
elt.thomson.com/destinations

Teacher site resources include:

- an answer key for each unit
- additional unit writing prompts, which can be used for in-class timed writings
- feedback sheets for teachers to use with student drafts of their writing (A complete explanation of these can be found on the Website.)
- evaluation/grade sheets for final drafts (A complete explanation of these can be found on the Website.)
- sample student paragraphs

Student site resources include:

- word parts (stems, prefixes, suffixes) exercises
- word forms (different forms of words in the reading—i.e., nouns, verbs, and adjectives)
- vocabulary quizzes (one for each unit)

Both teacher and student site resources include:

- learning objectives
- glossary
- flashcards with pronunciation
- crossword puzzles
- concentration game
- additional writing activities
- Internet exercises

The U.S. Learning Experience

Content Area: Personal Development/Study Skills

Reading: How to Be a Student in a U.S. Classroom

Short Readings: Choosing and Scheduling Classes
Scheduling Guidelines
Preparing for Classes
Organizing and Planning for Classes
Finding a Good Place to Study
Susan's Test-Taking Tips
Getting Support in Your Classes
Support Across the Campus

Sentence-Writing Focus: Basic Sentence Patterns (subject + verb;
subject + verb + object)

Editing Focus: Fragments/Word Order

Writing Focus: Introduction to Paragraphs (Examples)
The Writing Process

PART 1   UNIT PREVIEW

Preview Activity: Course Expectations/ Classroom Behavior Questionnaire

A. *Mark each statement below True (T) or False (F) for schools and classes in the United States.*

GENERAL INFORMATION/CLASSROOM PROCEDURES

_____ 1. Each instructor establishes specific rules for his/her class, so some classes may have different rules than other classes.

_____ 2. Missing classes or arriving late to class on a regular basis will not be a problem.

_____ 3. In general, eating, drinking, and smoking are acceptable in the classroom.

INSTRUCTOR ROLES AND RESPONSIBILITIES

_____ 1. If an instructor is not formal and strict, students will not learn anything.

_____ 2. Instructors are available for questions during office hours and/or after class.

_____ 3. Instructors should tell students everything about the subject they are teaching.

_____ 4. Instructors may talk most of the class, or they may require student participation.

_____ 5. Instructors should give students extra chances when the students do not complete the work or fail.

STUDENT ROLES AND RESPONSIBILITIES

_____ 1. Students should meet with a counselor or advisor, so they can make a plan for their studies.

_____ 2. Students do not have to complete work they miss when they are absent or out of the classroom. If they miss a quiz or assignment, they don't have to worry about it.

_____ 3. Students don't have to work hard in English classes because they are not as important as other classes.

B. *Share your answers with a partner and/or the class. Do you all agree with each other about these answers?*

Quickwrite/Freewrite

Each unit in this book will include a quickwrite or freewriting activity in the preview section. For this activity, you will write for a few minutes without thinking about details such as organization, grammar, spelling, and punctuation. The purpose of these activities is to let you start thinking about a topic and write some ideas about it.

Write for five minutes about the following topic. Do not worry about grammar, spelling, or punctuation. Just write what comes to your mind about the topic.

- What rules in your present classes are different and/or strange to you? Do you feel comfortable in your school situation now? Why or why not?

PART 2   READING AND VOCABULARY

Reading

How to Be a Student in a U.S. Classroom

Attending school can be both wonderful and **challenging.** Instructors and students each have **goals** and **objectives** for their classes and educational experience. In addition, teachers have **expectations** about student behavior in the classroom. Each instructor may organize or manage his/her class in different ways, but there are some classroom expectations that are typical. Following are **guidelines** and **tips** to help students make school in the United States a positive and **successful** experience.

1. Know and understand each instructor's course rules and expectations. Most instructors provide a **syllabus** or class description for their students during the first week of class. Students should keep these in a safe place, such as a folder or binder, and look at them whenever necessary. The syllabus includes important information, including how to contact the instructor (phone number, e-mail address, or other method). Students should **take advantage of** the instructor's office hours and **feel free to** discuss any questions or problems they are having.
2. Do not be absent from class because regular attendance is very important.
   If a student is absent or misses any part of class, s/he **is responsible for** finding out about and **catching up on** the work. This means the student should be ready to **hand in** assignments or take any tests during the next class session.
3. Come to class **on time** and do not to leave before the class finishes.
   Most instructors start class on time, and they often **announce** important information at the beginning or end of a class. Leaving class, even for a short time, is not polite and may also cause students to miss important information.

4. Come prepared to each class.

   Students should arrive to each class session with all of the following: textbook(s), pens/pencils, and blank paper or a notebook. In addition, students should read and prepare all homework assignments and bring completed work to hand in when **due**.

5. **Pay attention** in class and be prepared to actively participate.

   Students should be ready to ask or answer questions or work in pairs or groups with classmates. Reading materials unrelated to the class, completing homework during class time (for any class), sleeping, or having private conversations with others in the class are all examples of unacceptable classroom behavior. In addition, most instructors expect cell phones and pagers to be turned off during class time. Students should also try not to make **disruptive** noises, such as packing their bags before the class ends.

Comprehension Check

A. Main Idea/Details

It is important to know the difference between a main idea and a detail in both reading and writing. A main idea is general information, but a detail is more specific information. Details usually support a main idea by giving more information about it. Read the following four sentences. Which one is the main idea, and which ones are details that support that idea?

a. One teacher may never allow late homework in his class.

b. Others may deduct points for any late or missing homework.

c. Different teachers may have different rules about homework in their classes.

d. Another teacher may accept late homework but no later than the next class session.

Sentence *c* is the main idea because it makes a general statement about teachers and rules for homework. The other three sentences give examples of rules students might find with different teachers.

For each group of sentences below you will find one main idea and three details. In the space next to each sentence, write **MI** *for main idea and* **D** *for detail.*

1. _____ a. Do not ask other students questions while the instructor is explaining something.

   _____ b. You should not answer your cell phone and leave class to talk.

   _____ c. Bringing lunch and eating it during class is not a good idea.

   _____ d. Some kinds of behavior are not acceptable in the classroom.

2. _____ a. It's a good idea to see the instructor during his/her office hour to ask questions.

_____ b. There are several things students can do to make sure they are successful in a class.

_____ c. They should review the syllabus and make sure they understand rules and requirements.

_____ d. Completing all the homework assignments is always important.

B. Understanding Details

Put a check (✔) next to each statement about acceptable behavior or something important to know for a class in the United States. If the statement is about something unacceptable or unimportant, leave the space blank.

_____ 1. coming to class regularly and on time

_____ 2. getting homework and assignments when you are absent

_____ 3. bringing most homework and assignments late

_____ 4. leaving class for a few minutes

_____ 5. coming to school without any pens or pencils

_____ 6. bringing the textbook and blank paper or a notebook to class

_____ 7. asking questions when the instructor asks if everyone understands

_____ 8. getting ready to leave at the end of the class while the instructor is still talking

Vocabulary Study

A. Below you will find an underlined vocabulary word from the reading in each sentence and four definitions or synonyms after that sentence. Circle the two choices that have the same meaning as the vocabulary word. Follow the example.

1. It is a good idea to speak with other people at school to get <u>tips</u> about how to be more successful in your classes.

   a. extra money   b. new books

   c. helpful information   d. advice

2. The instructor told the students to pay attention to the class rules and important dates in the <u>syllabus</u>.

   a. course outline   b. course textbook

   c. course summary   d. course number

3. The students became nervous when the instructor <u>announced</u> a surprise quiz at the beginning of class yesterday.

   a. kept a secret about   b. gave information publicly about

   c. told everyone about   d. told only a few students about

4. I will probably stay up late tonight because my history paper is <u>due</u> tomorrow, and I need to finish it.

   a. scheduled   b. required

   c. late   d. not expected

5. When the student came late to class, his entrance was very <u>disruptive</u> because everyone looked at him and watched him take his seat.

   a. unusual   b. helpful

   c. upsetting   d. disturbing

B. *Choose a definition/synonym from the following list for each of the underlined vocabulary words in the sentences. Write the letter of the answer on the line next to the sentence. One definition/synonym will fit two vocabulary words. The first one has been done as an example.*

   a. end direction/aim   b. things they think will happen

   c. ~~demanding/difficult~~   d. instructions

   e. having a positive outcome

___C___ 1. Going to a new school can be <u>challenging</u> because there may be new rules and ways of doing things there.

_____ 2. The <u>goal</u> of this class is to improve your ability to write academic English.

_____ 3. People usually have <u>expectations</u> about classes before they take them, but sometimes the classes are different and don't follow these expectations.

_____ 4. When an instructor gives <u>guidelines</u> for how to prepare something for class, it's a good idea to follow these.

_____ 5. When you have a specific <u>objective</u> for your future, it will probably be easy to choose classes.

_____ 6. Usually the most <u>successful</u> students come to class regularly, do all the assignments on time, and have good study habits.

C. *Idioms*

An *idiom* is a special kind of vocabulary because it is a specific expression of two words or more. The words in an idiom work together to have a special meaning. If you try to find the meaning of an idiom in a dictionary, you will probably have trouble. This is because the dictionary will give you the meaning of each word in the idiom, but it will probably not tell you the meaning of the whole expression.

EXAMPLE: The student was absent from class, so he had to *catch up on* the work he missed.

What do you think the expression *catch up on* means?

(*Answer is at the bottom of this page.)

Choose a definition/synonym from the following list for each of the underlined vocabulary words in the sentences. Write the letter of the answer on the line next to the sentence.

a. not late/at the correct time
b. make use of something
c. look at/listen carefully to
d. give/turn in
e. have a duty/be required to do something
f. be comfortable with

_____ 1. At the end of the exam, the instructor asked all the students to <u>hand in</u> their papers.

_____ 2. My report is due tomorrow, so I will work on it all day today to make sure I finish it <u>on time</u>.

_____ 3. Students are <u>responsible for</u> knowing the rules and expectations of each class they take.

_____ 4. Students should <u>take advantage of</u> any help they can get from the instructor or tutors, especially if the students are having trouble understanding the material.

_____ 5. The instructor told her class <u>to feel free to</u> call or e-mail her with questions, so many students contacted her about the assignment.

_____ 6. Two students were talking and didn't <u>pay attention to</u> the teacher's instructions, so they completed the assignment incorrectly.

Discussion/Writing

Your teacher will tell you to answer these questions in writing or through discussion.

1. Which of the guidelines and tips in the reading were new for you? Did any of them surprise you? Why or why not? What other rules or expectations have you experienced in your classes?
2. What classroom rules and expectations are you most comfortable with? Which ones are you not comfortable with? Explain your answers.

---

*make up lost work when you fall behind; complete work to be at the same level as everyone else

PART 3   WRITING SENTENCES— BASIC SENTENCE PATTERNS

Read the paragraph about choosing and scheduling classes and answer the questions that follow.

Choosing and Scheduling Classes

[1]Gabriela always chooses her classes carefully. [2]As a first step, she goes to a counselor or advisor each semester. [3]Together they make a plan for her education. [4]Gabriela received placement test results in subjects such as math and English, so she followed those results. [5]Therefore, she completed the basic classes before she took the higher level or more advanced ones. [6]In addition, Gabriela always thinks about the amount of work that she expects in her classes. [7]Then she does not sign up for too many courses or units. [8]She tries to take classes that begin and end at convenient times for her work and family schedules. [9]Her best class schedules also leave time for her to complete assignments for all her classes. [10]Sometimes she comes to school early in the day. [11]Other times she works until late at night on homework and other assignments. [12]Gabriela spends a lot of time planning her schedule, so she is always happy with the final result.

 ## Questions

1. Look at sentences 1 and 2. Underline the subject and verb of each of these. Now do the same for sentences 3 and 10. Circle any objects in these same four sentences.

2. What kinds of words are necessary to make a good sentence in English? (What is the minimum necessary for a good sentence?)

Sentence-Writing
Focus

Sentence Patterns:
subject + verb;
subject + verb + object

Explanation: Basic Sentence Patterns

1. Every sentence in English must have a subject (who or what the sentence is about) and information about that subject.

   EXAMPLES: Gabriela <u>goes to a counselor every semester</u>.
         subject   information about the subject

      Sometimes she <u>works until late at night on her assignments</u>.
          subject   information about the subject

2. Every sentence in English must have a subject and a verb.

> EXAMPLES: Gabriela goes to a counselor every semester.
> subject   verb
>
> Sometimes she works until late at night on her assignments.
> subject   verb

3. A sentence with one subject and verb combination is called a *simple sentence.* Always use a capital letter at the beginning and include punctuation at the end of a simple sentence. This end punctuation will usually be a period (.) or a question mark (?). Sometimes it might be an exclamation point (!) if the sentence is a strong statement.

   Gabriela goes to a counselor or advisor at the end of each semester.

   Where does Gabriela go at the end of each semester?

   She never makes a schedule without talking to a counselor about it first!*

NOTE: Sometimes we put smaller sentences together to make a larger sentence by combining simple sentences. This is why some sentences may have more than one subject-verb combination. You will learn more about this sentence combining in other units in this book.

> Gabriela spends a lot of time planning her schedule, so she is always happy with the final result.

4. Some sentences (but not every sentence) will have an object after the verb.

   Two typical patterns for sentences in English are:

   a. subject + verb   (S + V)

   > Gabriela goes to a counselor every semester.
   > subject   verb
   > S   V

   To is a preposition. There is no object in this sentence. There is nothing receiving the action of the verb in this sentence.

   > She works until late at night on her assignments.
   > subject verb
   > S   V

   b. subject + verb + object (S + V + O)

   > EXAMPLE: Gabriela chooses her classes carefully.
   > subject   verb   object
   > S   V   O

---

*Do not use the exclamation point very often. Use it only when a statement is very strong.

What does Gabriela choose carefully? Here *classes* receives the action of the verb *choose.*

They make a plan for her education.
subject verb   object
   S   V   O

5. Most sentences have more than just a subject and a verb (S-V) or subject, verb, and object (S-V-O).

   a. Often the subject will be the first word of a sentence, and other words follow the verb or object.

      Gabriela went to the counseling office last week.
         S   V

      They made a plan for her classes.
        S   V   O

   b. Sometimes other words will come before the subject. It is important to know how to find the subject and verb of a sentence because they make the core of that sentence.

      EXAMPLE: As a first step, students should go to a counselor or advisor.
                                      S   V

                 Together they can make a plan for the student's education.
                           S   V   O

   c. Other words do not usually go between the verb and the object.

      INCORRECT: They make together a plan for her classes.
                     S   V   O

      CORRECT: Together they make a plan for her classes.
                             S   V   O

6. Sometimes a subject will have more than one person or thing. This is called a *compound subject.* A verb should agree in number with the subject of the sentence.

   EXAMPLES: A student chooses basic classes before the advanced ones.
               simple subject verb

               Counselors and students choose classes together.
               compound subject   verb

Editing Focus

Sentence Fragments

7. **Important—Error to Avoid**
   Remember: A good sentence always needs both a subject and a verb.* If you write a sentence without one of these pieces, you are making a mistake called a *fragment.* A fragment is a piece of a sentence but not a complete sentence.

   INCORRECT: Should see an advisor. (no subject)
                   V   O

_____

*Some sentences may have a command or imperative verb form. (Example: *Choose your classes carefully.*) In these cases, the subject is an understood *you.* This means that the reader or listener knows the subject is *you,* so we do not need to include it in the sentence.

CORRECT: Students should see an advisor.
                 S   V   O

INCORRECT: She always her class schedule carefully. (no verb)
                 S   O

CORRECT: She always chooses her class schedule carefully.
                 S   V   O

Practice: Sentence Patterns

A. **Identifying Sentence Parts**   *Put a line under the subject and verb of each sentence below. Then circle any objects you find in these sentences. Follow the example.*

1. Often <u>counselors help</u> (students) with their plans of study. Many students make appointments to see their counselors each semester. In this way, students work with counselors to make appropriate plans for their future studies.

2. In many cases students talk to their friends about their classes and schedules. They should see a counselor or advisor as well. Counselors know the requirements for specific programs or degrees.

B. **Writing Sentences—Word Order**   *Using the information given under each line below, write complete sentences. Be sure to use correct word order, capitalization, and punctuation.*

1. _____
   classes / different students / in different ways / choose

2. _____
   may read / for a description / a school catalog / students / of each class / before registration

3. _____
   in the bookstore / specific classes / find / some students / textbooks / to learn about

4. _____
   an instructor's syllabus / may read / other students / to get more information / about the class / online

C. **Writing Your Own Sentences**   *Write five sentences about your classes or class schedule using at least two of the following words in each sentence. Use one verb and one noun from the lists below in your sentences. Do not use the same words more than one time in any of your sentences. Be sure to pay attention to correct word order, capital letters, and end punctuation. You should also add some of your own words in these sentences.*

VERBS:
wait   try   begin   hand in   succeed   announce   pay attention to

NOUNS:
goals   tips   syllabus   rules   homework   expectations   behavior

D. Finding Sentence Problems

1. *Each sentence below has one of the following problems:*
   - *incorrect word order*
   - *missing subject*
   - *missing verb*

Find the mistake in each sentence and correct it. Follow the example.

a.   *Students* Need to think about the level of difficulty of a class before registration.

b.   All students should about any prerequisites (requirements) for each of their classes.

c.   Students take sometimes higher level or specialized classes before the more basic ones.

d.   Then may not succeed in those more difficult classes.

2. *Below you will find a paragraph about making a class schedule, and each sentence has one mistake. Find three sentence fragments, three problems with capital letters, two word order problems, and two punctuation problems. Correct all these mistakes.*

Scheduling Guidelines

What should students think about in order to make their class schedules. they need to have enough time to attend all their class sessions. This way will not have absences. In addition, they should leave time in their schedules for traveling to those classes Then they will not late to class. Teachers assign often two hours of homework for every class hour. therefore, students must have enough time after work or family needs to study and complete assignments. Finally, Students should not schedule their classes back-to-back (one right after another). This kind of class schedule affects sometimes study times or makes students too tired to study after class. Can make better schedules for themselves when they think about all these things.

Discussion/Writing

Your teacher will tell you to answer these questions in writing or through discussion.

1. When is the best time of the day or week for you to take classes? What is your ideal or perfect schedule for classes? Explain your answer.

2. What do you like most or least about your present schedule? How can you improve it?

PART 4   WRITING—INTRODUCTION TO PARAGRAPHS (USING EXAMPLES)

Paragraph Format

Look at the following piece of writing. Does it look like a paragraph? Why or why not? Write your answers on the lines provided.

preparing for classes.
Students can prepare for each class session in several ways. First
, they should establish a plan or study routine to follow.
This will make sure they prepare for each class on a regular basis.
Reviewing the class syllabus and calendar will help students decide more
specifically what to prepare for each class. This can also help students plan
to study for future lessons and tests.
In addition, completing each homework assignment on time is very important. Students should always complete all assigned readings, so they
will fully understand the lesson and be ready to participate in class
discussions or assignments.
Good students take notes during class and then go over those notes at
home. They also might review the information in the textbook after each
class lesson. In this way they can make sure they are ready to start the
new material for the next lesson.
Coming to class prepared from the last class and ready for the next will
help students succeed every time.

_____

_____

_____

Paragraph Discussion—Format

1. What is a paragraph?
   • A *paragraph* is a group of sentences about one topic or main idea. Usually there is a title and then a group of sentences below that.
2. What should a paragraph look like?
   Look at the paragraph about preparing classes in a different format.

Writing Focus
Paragraph
Titles and Format

`title`   Preparing for Classes

`indent`   Students can prepare for each class session in several ways. First, they should establish a plan or study routine to follow. This will make sure they prepare for each class on a regular basis. Reviewing the class syllabus and calendar will help students decide more specifically what to prepare for each class. This can also help students plan to study for future lessons and tests. In addition, completing each homework assignment on time is very important. Students should always complete all assigned readings, so they will fully understand the lesson and be ready to participate in class discussions or assignments. Good students take notes during class and then go over those notes at home. They also might review the information in the textbook after each class lesson. In this way they can make sure they are ready to start the new material for the next lesson. Coming to class prepared from the last class and ready for the next will help students succeed every time.

Notice the following changes in this paragraph:

A. Title

- The title is above the paragraph and centered on the page.
- Most of the words in the title begin with a capital letter. Only smaller words, such as articles (*a/an/the*) and prepositions (*for/on/at*) should not begin with a capital letter. There is one exception to this. The first word of a title should always be a capital letter, even if it is a small word like *a* or *for*.
- There is no period at the end of a title. (See the next section for more information about titles.)

B. Spacing

- The paragraph begins with a space before the beginning of the first sentence. This is called *indenting*. When you indent, you show the reader the start of a new paragraph.
- On the left and right sides of a paragraph there should be spaces to the edge of the paper. These spaces are called *margins*. The left margin should be the same for all lines. The right margin may not be exactly the same for every line when you handwrite a paragraph. When you type, you can left and right <u>justify</u> your work to make it even in the margins. There will also be top and bottom margins.

- Each sentence in the paragraph follows another. *Do not begin a new line with each new sentence.* Your sentences should not look like a list.
- Teachers often ask students to leave spaces between the lines in their writing. This is called *double spacing.* When you type, you can use the double space feature on the computer. When you write (by hand), you can skip a line between the lines you write.

C. Punctuation

- Be sure to keep end punctuation (periods, question marks, exclamation points) and commas on the line with the word they follow. Do not start a new line with one of these.

3. What should a title say?

   A title should give a general idea about the information in the paragraph. It tells the reader the main idea and can be as short as one word: *Studying,* or it can include several words: *My Study Routine.* A title is usually not a complete sentence or question.

Practice: Titles

Only one of the following titles follows all the rules just explained. Write "correct" on the line next to that title. For all the other titles, correct and rewrite them on the lines given.

1. The best place to study is the library.   _____
2. studying at home   _____
3. The Noise In The Dormitory   _____
4. Following a Regular Study Plan   _____
5. How Can I Study In My Noisy Apartment?   _____
6. My Study Routine.   _____

Practice: Paragraph Format

The paragraph below does not follow the rules about how a paragraph should look. On a separate piece of paper, rewrite or type this paragraph according to these rules. Be sure to use features of good paragraph form: correct spacing, margins, indenting, title placement.

Organizing and planning for classes
Successful students have different ways to stay organized and plan for classes.
   Organization can include paying attention to important dates for each class, such as deadlines for assignments or test dates. Students may mark these dates in their daily planners, on a wall calendar, or in electronic organizers.
   In addition, many serious students keep a "to-do" list. They can cross off completed tasks and add new ones to this list at any time.
Organizing notes and papers is also important for success in school. It is especially important not to lose papers, such as handouts that many teachers give separately in class. Many students keep these papers in folders or binders. Sometimes they create a system to keep these papers organized. For example
, they may keep them in the order that they received them from the teacher or in groups according to topics.
Organization and planning are important for success, so students should make sure they develop these skills for school.

Writing Focus

Paragraph
Organization:
Topic Sentences
and Details
(Controlling Ideas)

Paragraph Discussion—Organization

1. How should a paragraph begin?

   • In the reading comprehension in Part 2, pages 4 and 5, you learned about main ideas and details. Often the first sentence of a paragraph tells the reader the main idea. This sentence is called the *topic sentence*.

2. What about other sentences in the paragraph?

   • The other sentences in the paragraph are details. They give more information about the main idea. These details may be different kinds of information such as examples, facts, and reasons. These sentences are called *support* or *supporting sentences*.

   • The last sentence in a paragraph is often a *conclusion* or *concluding sentence*. This sentence is again more general. (You will learn more about conclusions in Unit Three.)

3. How many sentences or words should a good paragraph have?

   • There is no exact number of sentences or words for a good paragraph. You should have at least a topic sentence and several (at least 5 or 6) supporting sentences. A good paragraph develops and explains the main idea for the reader, so it should have enough details. Each of the paragraphs you will write for this class should have about 125 to 175 words.

Topic Sentences and Details

- A topic sentence is like the roof of a house. It covers everything below it. Just as the walls and rooms of a house support the roof, details support a topic sentence.

Look back at the paragraph on page 14 about preparing for classes. What is the topic sentence of that paragraph? Write it on the roof of the house below. What are the supporting details of this paragraph? Write them in the rooms of the house below. The first one has been done for you.

TITLE: _____

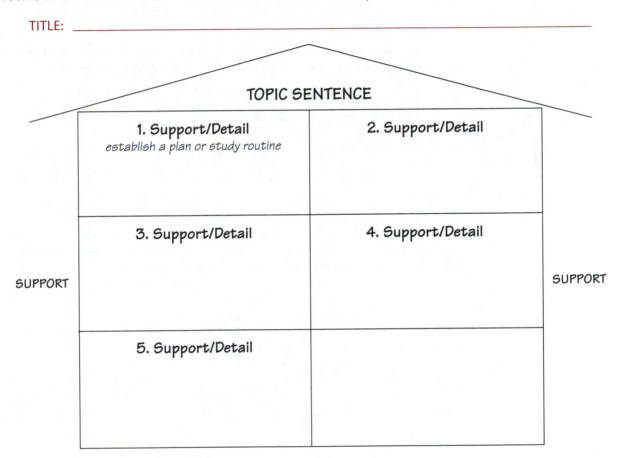

TOPIC SENTENCE

1. Support/Detail	2. Support/Detail
establish a plan or study routine	
3. Support/Detail	4. Support/Detail
5. Support/Detail	

SUPPORT   SUPPORT

Topic Sentences

A topic sentence is important because it tells the reader what the paragraph will be about. You learned about the two parts of a simple sentence (subject and information about the subject) in Part 3 of this unit. A good topic sentence will also have these two parts:

- a topic   This is the general idea or the subject of the paragraph.
- a controlling idea   This has information about the subject/topic of the paragraph. It tells the reader a specific part or aspect of that topic.

EXAMPLE TOPIC SENTENCE: Gabriela always chooses her classes carefully.
subject   controlling idea

The topic of this paragraph is Gabriela. There are many different paragraphs that someone could write about her, but this paragraph focuses on one part of her life. What information does the reader learn about Gabriela in this sentence?

Which of the following is that part of her life or the controlling idea?

- her job
- her childhood school experiences

- the way she chooses her classes
- her family life

Topics and Controlling Ideas

Think about this class as a topic. If someone asks you to write a paragraph about this class, what might you choose to write about?

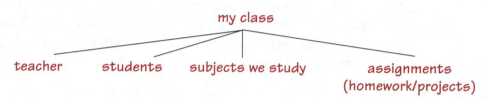

Do you think you could write one paragraph about all of these specific parts of your class? The answer is *probably not* because there is too much information in all of these to include in one paragraph. However, a writer could probably support each one of these with enough details to write a separate paragraph about each one:

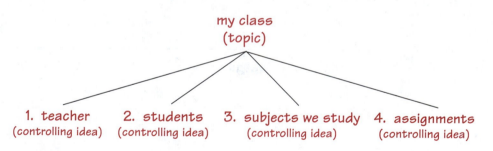

Practice: Topics and Controlling Ideas

A. Following are some example topic sentences for paragraphs about the topics in the diagram. Each of these topic sentences limits the topic even more. What is the controlling idea for each one?

1. The teacher in this class helps us practice our writing skills in different ways.

    Topic: teacher   **Controlling idea:**

2. The students in this class come from several different cultures.

    Topic: students   **Controlling idea:**

3. Some of the grammar topics in this class are very difficult to understand.

   Topic: grammar topics   **Controlling idea:**

4. Assignments in this class include homework, group projects, and computer lab work.

   Topic: assignments   **Controlling idea:**

B. Write two possible controlling ideas for each topic below.

1. college teachers _____

   _____

2. English teachers _____

   _____

3. college students _____

   _____

4. students from other cultures _____

   _____

Writing Good Topic Sentences

Topic sentences often include the writer's opinion, feelings, or other ideas that s/he can explain or describe in several sentences. In a good topic sentence the controlling idea is not too specific or too general.

1. If the controlling idea is too specific, the writer will not have enough to say in the paragraph. Usually a topic sentence will not be a simple fact because a simple fact may be too specific. Look at the following examples:

   • The name of the book in this class is *Destinations 1: Writing for Academic Success.*

   • This class meets five hours per week.

   What more can the writer say about the name of the book or how many hours a week the class meets? Probably there will not be enough information about these statements to write a good paragraph.

   Also, the topic sentence cannot be one detail from the paragraph. It should be general enough for all of the supporting sentences.

2. If the controlling idea is too general, the writer will have too much to say in one paragraph. Look at the following examples.

   • All the students in my class are taking different kinds of classes in addition to English.

   • Our teacher taught at several schools in different countries before she came to this one.

Paragraphs that follow these topic sentences will need too many supporting sentences to explain about all the students, all the classes, and all the schools in different countries.

Practice: Topic Sentences

A. Read the following titles and possible topic sentences for a paragraph about that topic. Put a check (✔) next to the best topic sentence for each one. Label the other sentences as too specific (TS) or too general (G).

1. TITLE: Getting Support in Your Classes

____ a. My friend Joe worked with his teacher one time last semester.
____ b. Students can do many things to succeed in all of their classes each semester.
____ c. Students can work with their instructors and classmates to increase their chances of succeeding in school.

2. TITLE: Support Across the Campus

____ a. Schools provide services and support programs in dozens of ways.
____ b. Schools often provide programs and services to help students succeed in their classes.
____ c. Last semester I went to a tutor to study for a test.

3. TITLE: Finding a Good Place to Study

____ a. Students should think about several things in order to find a good place to study.
____ b. Students should study on the second floor of the library every day.
____ c. Students should think about where to study, when to study, and for how long if they want to be successful.

B. Each of the paragraphs below needs a topic sentence. Read each paragraph. Then choose the best topic sentence from the three that follow each paragraph.

1. Finding a Good Place to Study

Many people feel a library is the best place to study, but not everyone can go there very often. A good study area at home will probably not be in a place for doing other things. For example, it may not be a good idea to choose a kitchen or a room with a television. Also, the study area should be comfortable and without distractions. It should have a comfortable desk and chair and enough room for supplies such as books and papers. In addition, good lighting is important. It is usually very difficult to study if there is not enough lighting to read texts and notes. Some people may want to talk to roommates or family members about keeping certain "quiet times" in the house or apartment. Others may even put up a "Please Do Not Disturb" sign on a door to inform people that they are studying. Students are responsible for much studying and preparation for classes, so they should be sure to find an appropriate place to do these things.

a. Most people do not try to find a specific place to study on a regular basis.

b. Students should consider several things in order to find a good place to study.

c. Many students study in the library.

2. Susan's Test-Taking Tips

For one thing, she read the instructions carefully and made sure to understand each question. When she had a question about a word problem, she asked the instructor about it. Also, she tried to use her time wisely. She quickly looked ahead at all the problems to see how many questions there were on the whole test. In addition, she did not spend too much time on any one problem. If she did not know how to do one, she skipped it and went on to the next one. Then, after she solved all of the easier ones, she went back to the more difficult ones. In the end Susan was very happy about using these tips because she received an A on that test.

a. During a difficult math test last week, Susan followed some test-taking tips she learned in her Study Skills 98 class.

b. Susan made sure she understood all the instructions and questions on the test.

c. Every time Susan takes a test for any class, she uses test-taking tips she learned in her Study Skills 98 class.

C. *Look back at your controlling ideas for Practice B on page 19. Write a topic sentence for each controlling idea in that activity. Be careful not to make your sentences too specific or too general.*

Support: Providing Examples

Read the following paragraph and answer the questions that follow.

Getting Support in Your Classes

Students can work with their instructors and classmates to increase their chances of succeeding in school. For one thing, they should understand that instructors are available for questions and extra help. For example, students can visit instructors during office hours or make an appointment to see their instructors at other times. In addition, finding

a "buddy" in the class is another kind of support. You may want to work with this person on homework and other assignments, or you can contact him/her just to ask questions. Also, students can form a study group with other students in the class. Often students in these groups work together outside their class. At these study sessions they review their notes, exchange opinions about materials and assignments from the class, and help each other with questions or in weak areas of understanding. Students should try to take advantage of some of these ways to help themselves in their classes.

1. Look at the topic sentence. What is the controlling idea? What kinds of examples do you expect to find in this paragraph?

2. There are three examples of how students can get support from instructors and classmates. What are these examples?

    a. _____

    b. _____

    c. _____

3. After each of the three examples, you can see one or two other sentences. What kind of information do you find in those other sentences? Why did the writer include those sentences?

4. Find the following words and expressions in the paragraph above:
    for one thing / for example / in addition / also
    What do these words and expressions mean? Why did the writer use them? What punctuation do you see after each of these?

Paragraph Discussion—Using Examples for Support

1. A good paragraph has several supporting sentences. These sentences give details about the topic sentence. Often these details are examples.

2. It is a good idea to include more than one sentence for each example in order to have enough support in a paragraph. In this way the writer can explain more about each example.

3. Writers may also use words and expressions called *transitions*. Transitions in an example paragraph often tell the reader several things as follows:

examples:	for example, for instance
the first example:	for one thing
another example:	in addition, also

Use these transitions at the beginning of a sentence and use a comma after each one.

4. The house below shows the organization of the sample paragraph as well as the transitions in it.

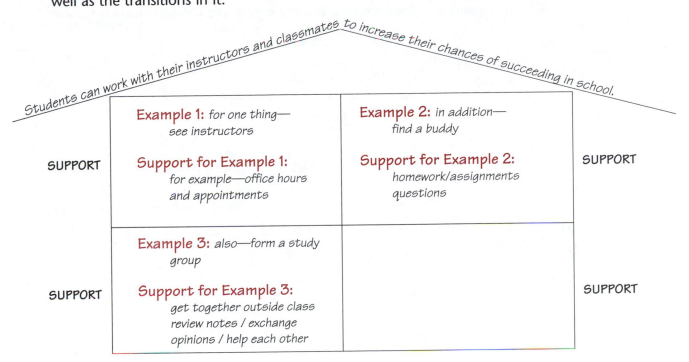

Students can work with their instructors and classmates to increase their chances of succeeding in school.

SUPPORT

Example 1: *for one thing— see instructors*

Support for Example 1: *for example—office hours and appointments*

Example 2: *in addition— find a buddy*

Support for Example 2: *homework/assignments questions*

SUPPORT

Example 3: *also—form a study group*

Support for Example 3: *get together outside class review notes / exchange opinions / help each other*

SUPPORT

SUPPORT

Practice: Supporting Paragraphs with Examples

A. Identifying Parts of a Paragraph

Read the following paragraph. Then fill in the spaces in the chart below it with information from the paragraph. Add any transitions (for one thing / in addition / also / for example / for instance) as well. (Use the chart above as a model.)

Support Across the Campus

Schools often provide programs and services to help students succeed in their classes and reach their goals. For instance, many schools offer tutoring in specific subjects. This service may even be free, and it often involves working individually or in a small group with a tutor. In addition, many schools have special labs or skills centers, such as a math lab or an English writing center. Usually students can get help from other students or get extra practice in specific subjects using computers in these labs and centers. Some students may prefer to use other kinds of equipment or technology to study, and many schools have these available as well. For example, students may learn from tapes, CDs, or DVDs, and schools often have special labs or programs that allow students to study with those. Students should always look for these kinds of resources at their school and make sure to use them as much as possible.

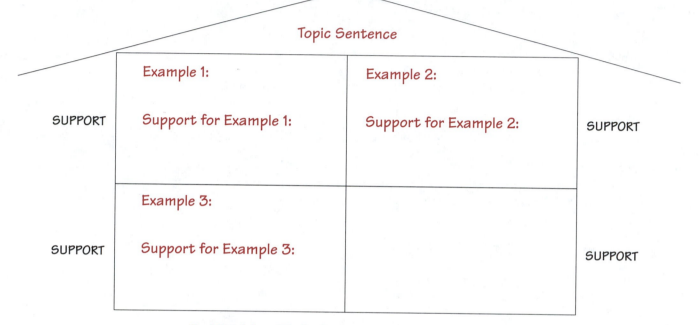

B. Matching: Topic Sentences and Examples
Match each topic sentence on the left with an example that fits from the column on the right. In some cases, two answers may be correct. Use each answer only one time.

A	B
1. A library/Learning Resource Center is a rich source of help for students in many ways.	a. practice trying to remember without the book in front of you
2. My friend gave me some helpful tips about studying for tests.	b. join clubs on campus
3. Yesterday we learned some ways to improve our memory for material we learn.	c. get help from librarians
4. For many students it is important to have a life outside their classes.	d. get up early in the morning to review

C. Examples to Fit Topic Sentences
Below you will find each topic sentence from Exercise B above and several possible examples for that paragraph. Cross out the one example in each group that does not fit.

EXAMPLE: Schools often provide programs and services to help students succeed in their classes and reach their goals.
  a. tutoring
  b. ~~study groups outside the class with classmates~~
  c. labs and skills centers
  d. other equipment or technology, such as CDs and DVDs

1. A library/Learning Resource Center is a rich source of help for students in many ways.
   a. tours of the library are available
   b. teachers leave special books on reserve or limited loan
   c. some students don't have time to go to the library
   d. online databases are available for research through the library

2. My friend gave me some helpful tips about studying for tests.
   a. bring the textbook and paper to every class session
   b. don't wait until the night before to begin studying
   c. don't stay up all night/get a good night's sleep
   d. plan ahead/don't cram (try to do everything in a short amount of time)
   e. find out as much as possible before the test and study what the instructor suggests

3. Yesterday we learned some ways to improve our memory for material we learn.
   a. make note cards of important or difficult information
   b. study/review notecards often
   c. remember important words (key words)
   d. highlight important information in the textbook
   e. make sure to know the dates of all assignments

4. For many students it is important to have a life outside their classes.
   a. relax and have fun on weekends
   b. get involved with community activities
   c. ask for extra credit work for each class
   d. make sure to forget about school after studying

Discussion/Writing

Your teacher will tell you to answer these questions in writing or through discussion.

1. What kinds of support or helpful services do you know about at your school? How can you find out more about these services or about others on campus?

2. What is your most successful way to study? Do you have any other tips or guidelines (in addition to those in this unit) about how to study for or take a test?
3. Do you think you spend enough time studying and preparing for your classes? Why or why not? What activities do you participate in outside the classroom?

Writing Assignment

Picking the Topic

Choose one of the following questions and write a paragraph that answers it. Be sure to include a topic sentence and examples to support it. Do not give reasons, just the examples. Be sure to explain your examples with more information.

1. What three or four important things does a new student at your school need to know about taking classes and studying there?
2. What three or four things do you think about when you make a new class schedule?
3. What are three or four ways you can improve your studying (study habits)? If you think you don't need to improve them at all, what are three or four of your most successful study habits?

The Writing Process

Most writers do not write perfectly the first time they try. Writing is a series of steps to follow. For each assignment in this book, you will follow these steps when you write your paragraphs.

Step One: Thinking about the topic/getting ideas

Step Two: Organizing your thoughts and ideas

Step Three: Getting someone else's opinion about your ideas (called *feedback*)

Step Four: Writing a first try (called a *first draft* or *rough draft*)

Step Five: Getting feedback about your draft

Step Six: Making changes

Step Seven: Writing the paragraph again (called a *final draft* and usually for a grade)

Following the Steps in the Writing Process

Before You Write

■ *Step One: Thinking about the Topic/Getting Ideas*
First, think about the three possible writing assignments. What ideas do you have for each topic? Write as many ideas as you can in the spaces below. You do not need to write complete sentences and don't worry about organization for this part. Follow the example below for a paragraph about how to improve your memory for things you learn in your classes.

Improving My Memory of Class Material

think of examples	write notes in the margin of the text
highlight things in textbook	practice remembering without the book
remember key words	make up little songs
make note cards	study note cards when waiting in line

Important Things for a New Student at My School

Making My Class Schedule

Improving My Study Habits

Now choose one of these topics to write your paragraph about. Make sure you have three or four ideas for the topic you choose.

■ *Step Two: Organizing Your Thoughts and Ideas*

Think about the main idea of your paragraph.

Topic Sentence

a. What is your topic? Are you writing about a new student, making your class schedule, or your study habits?

Topic: _____

b. What is your controlling idea? Which part of the topic do you want to develop in your supporting sentences? Will you write about important information for a new student, things you think about for your schedule, or improvements for your study habits?

Controlling idea: _____

c. Write your topic sentence on the chart at the end of this unit (page 31).

Support

d. Look back at your notes for Step One and circle the details you want to include. Make sure your paragraph has enough details. Make sure the details fit your topic sentence.

e. Write your ideas for support on the chart at the end of this unit (page 31).

f. Write a title for this paragraph on the chart at the end of this unit (page 31).

■ *Step Three: Getting Feedback about the Chart*
When you get feedback, you show your work to another person. This person usually tells you what is good about your work and what you can improve. For this part you will show your chart to another person. Your teacher may ask you to work with a partner and complete a review of your chart/outline. Use the review sheet in the Appendix (page 191) for this feedback.

When You Write

■ *Step Four: Writing the First Draft (Rough Draft)*
When you write a rough draft, it is the first time you try to write the complete paragraph. For this part, you should try to answer the questions and follow the directions of what to include in the paragraph. You should try your best but do not worry about perfect grammar, spelling, punctuation, or capitalization for this draft. Write the first draft of your paragraph using the ideas on the chart/outline (page 31).

Make sure to do all of the following in your rough draft:

Write a title.

Begin the paragraph with your topic sentence.

Write three or four examples to support your topic sentence.

Write at least one sentence to support each example.

Use at least three of the transitions from this unit at the beginning of your sentences.

Use at least three vocabulary words from this lesson.

After You Write

Check Your Work
After you finish writing the first draft, read your paragraph again. Check your work for the following. Do this before you show it to anyone else.

☐ This paragraph discusses one of the following:

- important information for new students
- making my class schedule
- study habits to improve (or successful study habits)

☐ This paragraph has a title.

☐ This paragraph has a topic sentence.

☐ This paragraph has three or four examples.

☐ All of the examples are about the topic sentence.

☐ I added more information about each example.

☐ I used three transitions at the beginning of sentences.

☐ I used three vocabulary words from this lesson in the paragraph.

☐ I checked my sentences for fragments (missing subjects or verbs).

This paragraph has correct paragraph form as follows:

☐ The title is centered above the paragraph.

☐ The title has correct capitalization.

☐ The title does not end in a period.

☐ I indented the first sentence of the paragraph.

☐ I have correct margins on the left and right.

☐ I did not put punctuation (period, comma, question mark) at the beginning of a new line.

☐ I double-spaced (skipped a space after every line).

☐ All of my sentences follow one another. (I did not go to the next line with a new sentence.)

■ *Step Five: Getting Feedback about the First Draft*
In this step you show someone your first draft of the paragraph. Your teacher will decide the type of feedback you will receive for the first draft. It may be with a partner or from the teacher or both ways. For review with a partner, use the sheet on page 190 in the Appendix.

■ *Step Six: Making Changes*
After you receive feedback, you should make changes. First, decide if you want to change your topic sentence. Also, think about your examples. Perhaps you want to take one or two out, or add a new one, or change the order. After you make these changes, look at all the grammar, punctuation, spelling, and capitalization. Make any necessary changes in these things as well.

■ *Step Seven: The Final Draft*
A final draft is usually the last time you write the paragraph before you give it to the teacher for a grade. You should type this draft on a computer. Try to make this paragraph as perfect as you can.

Organizing Your Thoughts for Writing

TITLE: _____

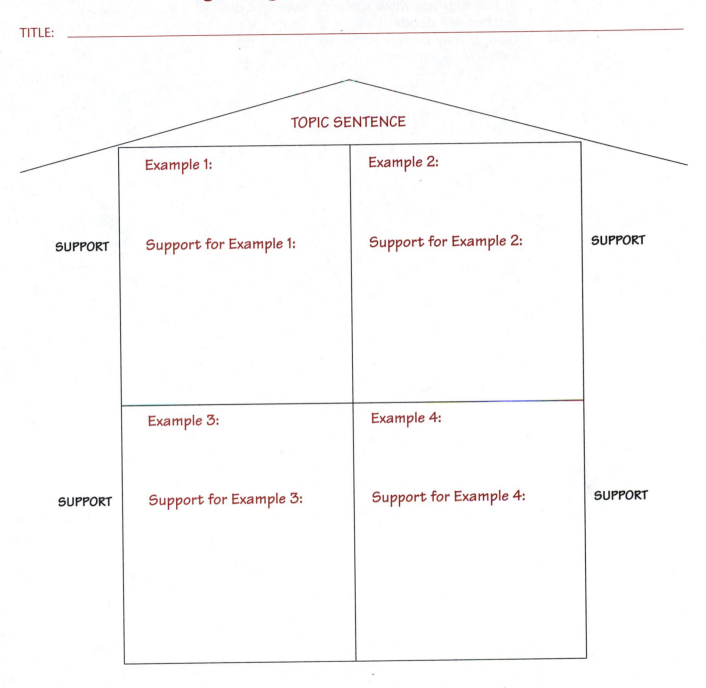

Body Decoration and Culture

Content Area: Cultural Anthropology

Reading: Body Decoration

Short Readings: Reasons for Body Art
Henna and Bridal Celebrations
The Wodaabe Geerewol Ceremony

Sentence Writing Focus: More Sentence Patterns (Subject + Linking
Verb + Adjective/Noun/Preposition and
There as Subject)

Editing Focus: Fragments/Word Order

Writing Focus: Paragraphs (Description)

PART 1   UNIT PREVIEW

Preview Activity: Discussion Questions and Body Decoration Recognition

A. Discuss the following questions with your teacher and classmates. Anthropology is a scientific study of people. Specialists in this area are called anthropologists. What exactly do anthropologists study about people? What is culture? How do you think it is related to anthropology?

B. How much do you know about body art or decoration in different cultures? Match each photo below with the information that fits it. Do you know why people use this kind of art/decoration on their bodies?

a. Henna designs on a Hindu bride's hands (India)

b. North American woman in heavy makeup

c. Japanese man with Irezumi tattoos

d. Tribeswoman from Ethiopia Omo river region with elongated lip and ear disks

e. Maori warrior from New Zealand with tattoos

Share your answers with a partner and/or the class. Share any other information you may have about the people and the body art in the photos.

Quickwrite/Freewrite

Write for five minutes about the following topics. Do not worry about grammar, spelling, or punctuation. Just write what comes to your mind about the topics.

• Do people in your native culture use any of the same kinds of body art or decoration you saw in the photos above? If so, which ones do they use? When and why do they use them?

• What other kinds of body art/decoration do you see on people in your native culture?

PART 2   READING AND VOCABULARY

Every culture throughout history practiced body art or body decoration, and this continues today. People do this for many different reasons, such as beauty, celebrations, rituals, and storytelling. Each society chooses its own way of making body art by using its own methods and materials as well as creating styles and traditions. There are many different kinds of body decorations, including body painting, tattooing, and piercing.

In the past many societies decorated their faces and bodies with different kinds of **removable** or **temporary** body painting. Centuries ago people made face and body paints with **natural materials,** such as **clay,** plants, and vegetable oil. In some parts of the world these old methods still continue today, but in the developed Western world, face and body painting are now part of the **cosmetics** business.

Tattooing is a **permanent** coloring/marking of the skin, usually of specific pictures or **designs.** Scientists found tattoos on 4,000- and 5,000-year-old **mummies,** and this kind of body art continues to be popular today. Tribal tattoos have been popular in many places around the world, such as Africa and the Pacific Islands for thousands of years. In fact, the word *tattoo* comes from the Tahitian (Polynesian) word *tatau.* To make a tattoo, someone **inserts** coloring into the skin with a **sharp** object. Sometimes tattoos are very colorful, but most often tattoos are black.

Piercing, or making a hole in the skin to insert objects, is another common way to decorate the body. In some societies piercing and decorating ears and lips with certain materials and colors can be very important. Many different things, such as bones, wood, feathers, and jewelry may decorate these pierced areas. Some groups of people wear special lip and ear **disks** or plates. Other people may use plugs to decorate the holes. These plates and plugs may be made of wood or other materials, and they often cause the area around the holes to become **stretched.**

People from many societies create **various** kinds of body art for many different reasons. Body art that is **attractive** to one culture may look strange or ugly to another. In addition, because of fashion changes even the makeup and hairstyles worn by one **generation** may look **unappealing** or old-fashioned to the next. These days some people in different parts of the world continue to follow their **traditional** kinds of body decoration, and others create new ones.

Comprehension Check

A. Main Ideas/Details

Which one of the following is the main idea of this reading? Circle the letter of your answer.

a. There are many reasons people in many parts of the world decorate their bodies.

b. Tattooing is a very old kind of body decoration, and it is still popular today all over the world.

c. People from different cultures and societies have practiced body decoration for many years in different ways.

*For each group of sentences below you will find one main idea and two details. In the space next to each sentence, write **MI** for main idea and **D** for detail.*

1. ____ a. One kind of popular body decoration is painting different parts of the body.

   ____ b. Some people use clay and plants to make materials for body painting.

   ____ c. Makeup and nail polish are two kinds of body painting.

2. ____ a. Some people tattooed their bodies 5,000 years ago.

   ____ b. The word *tattoo* comes from the Tahitian/Polynesian word *tatau*.

   ____ c. Tattooing is a coloring of the skin, and it stays on your body.

3. ____ a. Some people put bones and feathers in pierced areas of their body.

   ____ b. Some people pierce certain areas of the body and decorate them in different ways.

   ____ c. Lip and ear plates can make the pierced area bigger.

B. Understanding Details

Below and on the next page you will find a list of six details about the three kinds of body decorating in the reading: body painting, tattooing, and piercing. Write the numbers of the detailed information in the correct columns. One has been done as an example.

1. make a hole with a sharp object

2. decoration you can take off

3. pictures or designs under the skin

4. can be colorful but usually black

5. put a plug or plate inside a hole

6. use plants and oils to put colors on the body

Body painting	Tattooing	Piercing
		1

Vocabulary Study

A. *Below you will find an underlined vocabulary word from the reading in each sentence and four definitions or synonyms after that sentence. Circle the two choices that have the same meaning as the vocabulary word. Follow the example.*

1. On holidays people may perform a special <u>ritual</u> every time that day is celebrated.

    a. ceremony   b. body art

    c. sport   d. social custom

2. Many people use <u>cosmetics</u> on their face and skin in order to try to look younger.

    a. soaps   b. makeup

    c. beauty products   d. oils

3. Before you get a tattoo, you must choose the <u>design</u> you want the artist to make on your skin.

    a. color   b. kind of ink

    c. pattern   d. drawing

4. The old woman wore very heavy earrings for many years, so her ears <u>stretched</u> down.

    a. pulled out   b. increased

    c. got smaller   d. became painful

5. Some people think tattoos are very <u>attractive,</u> but other people do not like to look at them.

    a. ugly   b. good looking

    c. pleasant   d. strange

6. Sometimes young people do not want to be <u>traditional,</u> so they do things differently than their parents.

    a. customary   b. helpful

    c. usual   d. unusual

7. My friend has a tattoo with <u>various</u> colors because he didn't want it to be all black.

a. equal

b. several kinds of

c. bright

d. different

B. *Choose a definition/synonym from the following list for each of the underlined vocabulary words in the sentences. Write the letter of the answer on the line next to the sentence. The first one has been done as an example.*

a. able to take away
b. ~~earthy material~~
c. having an edge or point to cut
d. put into or inside
e. preserved dead bodies
f. people of the same age group
g. not attractive or pleasing
h. continuing with no change

_b_ 1. People often use <u>clay</u> to make pottery, such as plates and bowls.

____ 2. Many women in this country use <u>removable</u> makeup on their eyes each day.

____ 3. Some women have <u>permanent</u> lines put around their eyes, so they don't have to put on makeup every day.

____ 4. Some ancient cultures purposely made <u>mummies,</u> but sometimes natural things, such as ice and sand created them.

____ 5. Jenna pierced her ears yesterday. Then she <u>inserted</u> her earrings into the holes very carefully.

____ 6. The box was difficult to open, so Joe used a <u>sharp</u> knife to cut it open.

____ 7. People of a younger <u>generation</u> often want to do things differently than their parents.

____ 8. People have different ideas of beauty. One person may like a certain kind of makeup and another person may find that <u>unappealing</u>.

C. Context Clues

Sometimes you may see an unfamiliar word when you read. It may not always be necessary to look for this word in a dictionary. You might be able to understand the new word from other parts of the sentence. Two ways you can do this are:

a. Look for the definition or a synonym (word with the same meaning) right after the unfamiliar word.

EXAMPLE: What does the word *piercing* mean in the following sentence?
Piercing, or making a hole in the skin to insert objects, is
another common way to decorate the body. After the word
or you can see the meaning of piercing (*making a hole in the
skin to insert objects*).

b. Look for examples or a division into parts of the unfamiliar word to
help you understand its meaning.

EXAMPLE: What does *decorations* mean in the following sentence?
There are many different kinds of body *decorations*, including
body painting, tattooing, and piercing.

Body painting, tattooing, and *piercing* are examples of decorations. Many
people wear these things to add beauty. You can guess the meaning of
the word *decorations* is about beauty from these examples.

*What do the underlined words in the following sentences mean? Use context
clues in the sentences to help you with your answers. Do not use a dictionary
for this activity.*

1. In the past many societies decorated their faces and bodies with
different kinds of removable or <u>temporary</u> body painting.

2. Centuries ago people made face and body paints with <u>natural
materials</u>, such as clay, plants, and vegetable oil.

3. Some groups of people wear special lip and ear <u>disks</u> or plates.

Discussion/Writing

*Your teacher will tell you to answer these questions in writing or through
discussion.*

1. Do you see all three kinds of body decoration (body painting,
tattooing, and piercing) in your everyday life? Where do you usually
see people with these? Which kinds are the most popular?

2. Why do you think tattoos and piercings are popular with so many
people today in many countries?

PART 3   WRITING SENTENCES—
MORE SENTENCE PATTERNS

Read the paragraph about body art and answer the questions that follow.

Reading

Reasons for
Body Art/
Decoration

[1]There are many reasons for practicing body art. [2]Often body decoration is an important way for people to show artistic expression. [3]Many
people feel attractive to others with body art. [4]It is sometimes the only

way for nomadic people* to keep their art with them. [5]They can move from place to place, and still have their art with them at all times. [6]Some people wear body art as part of a special group or for religious reasons. [7]Other times people use it in warfare. [8]With face and body decorations, warriors seem stronger or fiercer to their enemies. [9]Some decorations are special for certain people. [10]For example, the Maori chiefs of New Zealand wore detailed tattoos on their faces, called *Ta Moko*. [11]For them their identity or character was in the *Ta Moko* designs. [12]A design was very important to each chief, so he drew it on important documents as his signature.

Questions

1. Look at sentences 6, 7, and 10. Circle the subject and verb of these sentences. Put a line under any objects you find in these three sentences.

2. a. Look at sentence 2. Circle the three words that come immediately after the word *is.* What kind of information did you circle? (What does this information tell you?)

   b. Look at sentence 9. Circle the word that comes immediately after the word *are.* What kind of information did you circle? (What does this information tell you?)

   c. Look at sentence 11. Circle the information that comes after the word *was.* What kind of information did you circle? (What does this information tell you?)

3. Circle the subject and verb in sentence 1.

Sentence-Writing
Focus

More Sentence
Patterns: Linking
Verbs with
Adjectives,
Prepositions,
and Nouns;
There as Subject

Explanation—More Sentence Patterns

1. As you learned in Unit One, every simple sentence must have at least a subject and a verb, but usually there will be other words in the sentence as well. A simple sentence may follow the subject + verb + object pattern, or it may not have an object.

   EXAMPLE: Maori chiefs lived in New Zealand.

                      S   V   (no object)

   They wore detailed tattoos on their faces.

   S   V   O

*people who move from place to place

2. Some other sentence patterns are also very common in English, and they include verbs known as *linking verbs*. *Be* (*is/am/are/was/were*) is the most common linking verb. Some other linking verbs are: *seem   feel   look   become   sound   taste   smell.* Sentences with linking verbs do not have objects. They follow the subject + verb pattern.

3. The information after linking verbs is usually one of three types:
    a. adjective—a word that describes

    EXAMPLES: Some decorations *are special* for certain people.
    adjective

    Many people *feel attractive* to others with body art.
    adjective

    b. noun/identification (tells who or what something *is*)

    EXAMPLES: Often body decoration *is an important way* for people to
    show artistic expression.   noun (identifies body
                                        decoration/tells what it is)

    The Maori man with the detailed tattoos on his face *was
    a chief.*
    noun (identifies the man)

    c. preposition*/location (prepositional phrase*)

    EXAMPLES: Their character or personality was *in those designs.*
                                    preposition/location = *in*
                                    prepositional phrase = *in those
                                    designs*

    The Maori men with the tattoos *are from New Zealand.*
                                preposition/location = *from*
                                prepositional phrase = *from
                                New Zealand*

NOTE: Prepositional phrases do not contain the subject or object of a sentence. Be careful when you have a prepositional phrase between the subject and verb or at the beginning of a sentence. Also, a sentence may have more than one prepositional phrase.

EXAMPLES: With face and body decorations, warriors seem fiercer
           prepositional phrase   subject   verb
           to their enemies.
           prepositional phrase

           An important tattoo for a Maori chief was on his face.
           S   prepositional phrase V   prepositional phrase

---

*A preposition is one word, such as *on, for, in, at, to, from.* A prepositional phrase is two words or more. It includes the preposition and noun or pronoun after the preposition.

4. Another common sentence pattern begins with *there + be* (*is/are/was/were*). In this case the word *there* comes before *be,* and a noun follows *be.* The form of *be* must agree in number with the noun that follows it.

   EXAMPLES: There *are* <u>many reasons</u> for practicing body art.

   This *is* <u>a special tattoo</u> for Maori chiefs.

5. All of these sentence patterns follow the same rules you learned in Unit One about a capital letter at the beginning and end punctuation.

   An important tattoo for a Maori chief was on his face.

   Are Maori tattoos an important part of that culture**?**

   Tattoos for Maori chiefs were very special**!**

Editing Focus

Sentence Fragments

6. **Important—Error to Avoid**
   Remember: A good sentence always needs both a subject and a verb. Be careful about leaving out a piece of the sentence and making a *fragment.*

   INCORRECT: Were very special. (no subject)

   CORRECT: Face tattoos for Maori chiefs were very special.

   INCORRECT: An important tattoo for a Maori chief on his face. (no verb)

   CORRECT: An important tattoo for a Maori chief was on his face.

   INCORRECT: There many reasons for practicing body art. (no verb)

   CORRECT: There are many reasons for practicing body art.

Practice: Sentence Patterns—Using Linking Verbs and **There** *as Subject of a Sentence*

A. **Identifying Sentence Parts**   *Circle the subject and put a line under the verb of each sentence below. Then label the information in bold* A *for adjective,* N *for noun of identification, and* P *for prepositional phrase. (Remember: A subject will not be in a prepositional phrase.) The first one has been done as an example.*

1. a. In India an important (decoration) is often **on the forehead.** `P`

   b. A red mark on the forehead is a **mark** of marriage.

2. a. For some people body art became **a way** to communicate information.

   b. For example, sometimes disks are **in people's lips** as a message.

   c. In some places people with lip plates are good **speakers.**

   d. Other people with pierced lips were **successful** in war.

3. a. Body painting is often **temporary**.

   b. A popular temporary body painting is **henna**.

   c. A mixture of dried plants and different liquids becomes a **paste** for decorating the skin.

   d. Henna decorations are often **on the hands and feet**.

B. **Matching**   *Match the first part of each sentence in column A with information to follow from column B. In some cases more than one answer may be correct, but you should use each answer only one time.*

A	B
1. Some body decorations	a. often become larger.
2. In many societies some decorations of jewelry, wood, or bones	b. is self-expression.
3. Pierced lips with plates or disks	c. are a way to rebel.
4. There are	d. seem strange to people outside that society.
5. For some young people tattoos	e. specific kinds of lines on face tattoos in Melanesia.
6. For other people a tattoo	f. are on the ears or in the nose.

C. **Writing Sentences—Word Order**   *Using the information given under each line below, write complete sentences. Be sure to use correct word order, capitalization, and punctuation. Do not add or change any of the words.*

1. _____

   of North America / skilled face painters / were often / Native Americans

2. _____

   in battles / looked fierce and brave / warriors / with painted faces

3. _____

   from the sun and wind / was also / face painting / a kind of protection

4. _____

   ritual designs / on their foreheads and cheeks / for dances and ceremonies / were often

5. _____

   were usually / these designs / symbolic / and their colors

6. _____

   bright and bold / were often / the colors / in their paintings

D. **Writing Your Own Sentences**   *Look back at the photos in Part 1 of this unit. Choose one of these photos and write five sentences about what you see. All five of your sentences should be about the same picture. Follow the pattern given under each line.*

1. _____

Begin the sentence with *there is* or *there are*.

2. _____

Use a linking verb and an adjective.

3. _____

Use a linking verb and a noun of identification.

4. _____

Use a linking verb and a prepositional phrase of location.

5. _____

Use the subject-verb-object pattern.

Show your sentences to another student or group of students and you read their sentences. Guess which photo their sentences described, and they will guess the photo you described.

E. **Finding Sentence Problems**   *Each sentence below has one of the problems listed. Find the mistake in each sentence and correct it. Use any of the linking verb patterns or* there *as a subject to correct these sentences.*

Problems:

   • incorrect word order   • missing subject   • missing verb

1. Body art popular in many different societies.

2. With tattoos look different from other people.

3. Some people younger feel with makeup on their face.

4. Are important symbols in tattoos for some cultures.

5. Pierced nose decoration a symbol is of marriage and wealth.

6. In some societies lip plates a sign of beauty and wealth.

7. Is a special kind of face painting in Maori culture in New Zealand.

8. Colorful tattoos seem for some people.

9. Often white wisdom and understanding in body decorations.

Discussion/Writing

Your teacher will tell you to answer these questions in writing or through discussion.

1. The reading on pages 39 and 40 gave some reasons for body decorations. What other reasons do people have for body art?

2. Do you wear any kind of temporary or permanent body decorations? What is your opinion of tattoos and body piercings? Why do you feel this way?

PART 4   WRITING—PARAGRAPHS USING DESCRIPTION

Read the following paragraph about henna decorations and then answer the questions that follow it.

Henna and Bridal Celebrations

In some parts of the world, brides receive temporary tattoos of henna at special celebrations before their marriage. These parties are usually for women only, and they take place from one to several days before the wedding. During these celebrations a relative of the bride or a specialist in henna art (also called Mehndi) paints the hands and feet of the bride with detailed designs. The henna decorates the bride's skin and provides a good smell for her wedding night at the end of the day. The henna paste is dark brown or black, and it usually stays on the skin for eight hours or more. Then it becomes a dark red stain, and it can become darker as it stays on the skin for a longer time. While the bride is getting her henna decorations, the other women sing and dance traditional songs and dances. They may also paint their hands with henna, but their designs are smaller and simpler than the ones on the bride. Drawing henna decorations on a bride is an old tradition and an important custom for many people in different cultures.

Paragraph Discussion

1. Does this paragraph follow the correct paragraph format you learned in Unit One? Does it have all of the following?

    ___ a title centered above the paragraph

    ___ correct capitalization of the title

___ indenting of the first sentence

___ each sentence following the one before

___ correct left and right margins

___ a capital letter at the beginning of each new sentence

___ end punctuation for each sentence

2. Which sentence in this paragraph is the topic sentence? What is the topic and what is the controlling idea of this sentence?

3. What kind of information do the supporting sentences give?

Paragraph Organization—Using Description

The topic sentence of this paragraph tells the reader it will be about brides using a kind of temporary tattoo (henna) before their weddings. The supporting sentences describe the celebration and the henna tattoos. A good description helps the reader clearly "see" something. In order to do this, a writer uses several kinds of words to paint a vivid (clear) picture in his/her writing. Good descriptions often use different kinds of nouns, adjectives, and prepositional phrases. (See Part 3, page 41 for a review of these kinds of words with linking verbs.)

EXAMPLES:
• Adjectives: such as colors, sizes, feelings, appearance, other characteristics

Brides receive *temporary* tattoos at *special* celebrations. The henna paste is *black*.

• Nouns: such as numbers, names of people and places, things

These *parties* take place from *one* to several *days* before the *wedding*. The henna *paste* is also called *Mehndi*.

• Prepositions/Prepositional phrases

In some parts of the world, brides receive temporary tattoos *of henna at special celebrations before their marriage*.

• Things related to the senses: such as smells, sounds, and tastes

The henna provides *a good smell*.

Practice: Description

A. Finding Descriptive Words

In the example paragraph, the writer wants the reader to see vividly the use of henna at bridal celebrations. Look back at the paragraph and do the following:

a. Write the topic sentence on the line at the top of the following chart (the roof).

b. Find examples of words or expressions from the paragraph that fit the categories in the boxes below. Write the words and expressions you find in the appropriate boxes. Several examples have already been given.

HENNA AND BRIDAL CELEBRATIONS

NAMES (proper nouns) (people/places) *Mehndi*	**NUMBERS** *one*	**OTHER NOUNS** *parties* *days* *wedding* *paste*
COLORS *black*	**FEELINGS** (how people feel)	
SENSES (smells/sounds/tastes) *a good smell*	**PREPOSITIONAL PHRASES** *in some parts of the world of henna at special celebrations before their marriage*	**OTHER ADJECTIVES** *temporary* *special*

B. **Recognizing Vivid Descriptions** *Next to each number below you will see two descriptions. Decide which one is more vivid by putting a check (✔) on the line next to that description. What specific words make those sentences better descriptions?*

1. ____ Some natives of North America put things in their lips.

   ____ The Inuit people of North America made lip piercings by putting bone jewelry in their lips.

2. ____ Native Eskimos wore lip plugs called *labrets* made of ivory.

   ____ Some Native Americans wore lip plugs.

3. ____ Eskimo men wore labrets.

   ____ Eskimo men could wear one or two labrets when they became old enough.

4. ___ Eskimo women also wore a labret in their lip.

___ Eskimo women also decorated their lip by increasing the size of the hole with larger plugs.

C. **Writing Descriptive Sentences**   *Look back at the photos in Part 1 of this unit on page 34. Write two descriptive sentences for each photo. Be sure to use as many of the following kinds of words in your sentences as possible; colors, feelings, other adjectives, numbers, names, other nouns, senses, prepositional phrases.*

Review: Titles and Topic Sentences

Remember the following about a title:

- It gives the general idea of the paragraph in just a few short words (perhaps one to four or five words).

- It is usually not a complete sentence. It should not have end punctuation, such as a period.

- Most of the words in a title will begin with a capital letter. (See Unit One, page 14 for review.)

    EXAMPLE: Inuit Lip Piercings

Remember the following about a topic sentence:

- It is a complete sentence. It should begin with a capital letter and have end punctuation.

- It has a topic and a controlling idea. The topic is the general subject of the paragraph. The controlling idea limits the topic to something more specific about that subject.

    EXAMPLE: The Inuit people of North America wore lip piercings of bone jewelry.

Practice: Topic Sentences and Supporting Sentences Using Description

A. Identifying Topic Sentences and Supporting Details
*Read the following titles and sentences. For each group of sentences, label the topic sentence (**TS**) and the descriptive details (**D**) on the lines next to the sentences. The first one has been done as an example.*

1. TITLE: Brazilian Native American Body Painting

_D_ a. They use the red seeds of the plant to make a paste.

_TS_ b. Several groups of Native Americans in Brazil practice body painting using a plant called *urucu* or *annatto*.

_D_ c. They paint men, women, and even babies with this red paste.

_D_ d. The women wear a pale color, and the men wear a dark color for their decorations.

2. TITLE: Lip Decorations in Africa

___ a. During childhood they pierce a girl's lower lip and insert a small plate.

___ b. These plates are made of wood or clay.

___ c. For the Surman women in Africa, it is important to show their wealth and beauty with lip plates.

___ d. They slowly stretch the lip by inserting larger plates.

3. TITLE: Japanese Irezumi

___ a. These tattoos are very colorful designs and often cover the whole body.

___ b. A tattoo artist draws the design on the skin with a pen and then outlines each part of the tattoo with charcoal-based ink.

___ c. It may take one hundred hours of work to cover a body with these tattoos.

___ d. The very old Japanese art of tattooing called Irezumi is still popular today.

___ e. He fills in the colors with different shades by inserting the tattooing needles to different depths under the skin.

4. TITLE: Boys of the Txucarramae Tribe of the Amazon

___ a. They paint certain plants, such as palm leaves to make ear decorations.

___ b. They also wear lip disks made of lightweight wood called *sara*.

___ c. Their most important decorations are feathers from colorful birds in the forest, such as toucans.

___ d. Txucarramae boys of the Amazon wear body decorations of wood, plants, and feathers.

B. Identifying Topic Sentences and Descriptive Support

Follow the same directions as above. In addition, this time you should find one detail that does not fit the paragraph or topic sentence. It does not follow the description of the rest of the sentences. Put a line through that one sentence in each group. The first one has been done as an example.

Xingu man of the
Kamayura tribe in
the Brazilian
Amazon area.

1. TITLE: Body Painting of the Txicao

_D_ a. They paint their bodies with a paste from the urucu plant.

_D_ b. They also use charcoal and the blue-black juice of a native fruit (called *genipip*).

___ c. ~~In addition, they grow their hair long down to their shoulders~~.

_D_ d. They use these materials to make very complicated designs and patterns on their bodies.

_TS_ e. Txicao men in Brazil paint themselves using various natural materials.

2. TITLE: Australian Aboriginal Body Art

___ a. They use natural materials to make paint of different colors.

___ b. They often paint special designs and symbols on their faces and bodies.

___ c. Body art has always been important to the aboriginal people of Australia.

___ d. They often play native instruments at their ceremonies as well.

___ e. The designs are usually stripes, circles, and dots.

3. TITLE: Body Decoration in Papua New Guinea

___ a. For body and face painting they use different kinds of clay such as blue, white, and yellow river clay and a red coloring from a different kind of clay.

___ b. Papua New Guinea is an island in the Pacific Ocean.

___ c. The people of Papua New Guinea wear several kinds of body decorations.

___ d. They use different styles of face painting for men and women.

___ e. Women also may wear tattoos on their faces.

___ f. Men may pierce their noses and ears.

4. TITLE: Body Decoration of Tchikrin Children

___ a. When a boy is eight years old, he leaves his mother to live in a men's hut.

___ b. Fathers pierce the earlobes of their babies when they are born.

___ c. Then the babies wear red wooden ear disks.

___ d. The Tchikrin also pierce the lower lips of the baby boys with a string of beads.

___ e. The Tchikrin people of the Amazon decorate their children with piercings and body painting from birth.

___ f. Mothers and grandmothers paint designs of lines on the baby's body.

C. Identifying Parts of a Descriptive Paragraph

Read the following descriptive paragraph about a group of people in Africa and their particular kind of ceremonial body decoration. Then do two things:

1. Write the topic sentence on the line above the chart (the roof).
2. Fill in the chart with words and expressions from the reading. You may not have information for every box, but you should have some words for most of them.

The Wodaabe Geerewol Ceremony

The Wodaabe men of Niger Africa hold important celebrations called Geerewol for several days each year. At these celebrations the men perform special dances to display their charm and beauty. They prepare special costumes, makeup, and tattoos for hours before these dances. For the *Yaake* dance, the men put pale yellow powder on their faces in order to lighten their skin. They also apply black borders of a material called kohl around their teeth and eyes to make them seem very white. Then they make their nose look longer with a painted white line from their forehead to their chin. In addition, they shave the hairline at the top of their head so the forehead becomes higher than usual. For the dance, the men stand in a line and walk on their toes for extra height. The Wodaabe believe beauty is especially in the eyes, so for the yaake dance the men move their eyes by rolling them. Then they make strong facial expressions with their eyes, teeth, and cheeks. When Wodaabe men dance in the Geerewol celebrations, they show their charm and beauty hoping to attract a woman at the same time.

THE WODAABE GEEREWOL CEREMONY

NAMES (proper nouns) (people/places)	NUMBERS	OTHER NOUNS
COLORS	FEELINGS (how people feel)	
SENSES (smells/sounds/tastes)	PREPOSITIONAL PHRASES	OTHER ADJECTIVES

Discussion/Writing

Your teacher will tell you to answer these questions in writing or through discussion.

1. What special ceremonies or rituals using body art or decorations do people in your culture (or the culture you are now living in) celebrate? What is the reason for the body art in this celebration or ritual?

2. How do you feel about body decoration/art? What kinds are beautiful? What kinds are ugly to you? Why?

Writing Assignment

Picking the Topic

Choose one of the following three topics and write a descriptive paragraph about it. Be sure to include a topic sentence and descriptive details to support it. You should paint a picture with your paragraph so the reader can see what you are describing in his/her mind.

Describing body art/decoration
1. Describe a specific body decoration that you or a friend or family member has or uses often. This can be a temporary or permanent decoration. What exactly does this body art look like?

2. Describe a specific kind of body art or decoration from your culture. What exactly does it look like? Give a detailed description of what it looks like. It could be any of the kinds of body art/decoration discussed in this unit or a special kind of clothing. (Do not describe a ceremony that may be related to it.)

Describing a ceremony or celebration
3. Describe a ceremony or ritual from your culture that includes some kind of body art or decoration. Describe both the ceremony and the body art or decorations.

Practice with Description

Work with a partner or in a small group for the following activity.

- Choose one person in your classroom. Describe this person in a few short sentences (3 to 5 sentences). Do not tell the name of the person.
- Choose one object in your classroom and describe it in a few short sentences (3 to 5 sentences). Do not tell the name of this item.
- Share one of your descriptions with the other people in the class. They must guess the person or object you are describing.

> EXAMPLE: This object is in my kitchen.
> It is very cold on the inside.
> Sometimes it is very large, but sometimes it can be small.
> People keep food in it to keep the food fresh.
> (ANSWER: a refrigerator)

Following the Steps in the Writing Process

Before You Write

Step One: Thinking about the Topic/Getting Ideas
First, think about the writing assignments. What ideas do you have for each topic? Write as many ideas as you can in the spaces below. You do not need to write complete sentences and don't worry about organization for this part.

Describing My (or My Friend's or Relative's) Body Art

(continued)

Describing Body Art of My Culture

Describing a Ceremony with Body Art

Now choose one of these topics to write your paragraph about. Fill in the chart below with as many words and expressions about your topic as you can for each box.

TOPIC: _____

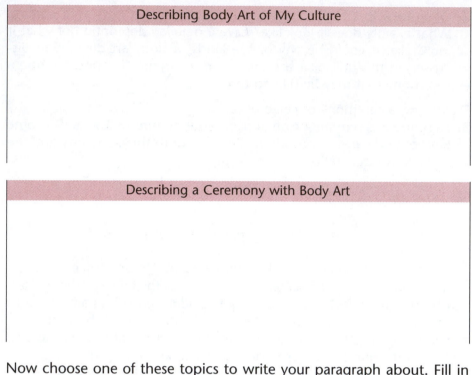

NAMES (proper nouns) (people/places)	NUMBERS	OTHER NOUNS
COLORS	FEELINGS (how people feel)	
SENSES (smells/sounds/tastes)	PREPOSITIONAL PHRASES	OTHER ADJECTIVES

■ *Step Two: Organizing Your Thoughts and Ideas*
Think about the main idea of your paragraph.

Topic Sentence

a. What is your topic? Are you going to write about your body art (or the art of a friend or relative), a kind of body art in your culture, or a celebration or ceremony that includes body art?

   Topic: _____

b. What is your controlling idea? What part of the topic will you describe in your supporting sentences?

   Controlling idea: _____

c. Write your topic sentence on the chart at the end of this unit (page 58).

Support

d. Look back at your notes and the chart of words and expressions for Step One and circle the details you want to include. Make sure your paragraph has enough details. Make sure the details fit your topic sentence and will give a vivid description.

e. Write your ideas for support on the chart at the end of this unit (page 58). You do not need to write complete sentences on this chart, but you should include specific words from the chart in Step One (page 53).

f. Write a title for this paragraph on the chart at the end of this unit (page 58).

■ *Step Three: Getting Feedback about the Chart*
Show your chart to another person. Your teacher may ask you to work with a partner and complete a review of your chart/outline. Use the review sheet in the Appendix (page 193) for this feedback.

When You Write

■ *Step Four: Writing the First Draft (Rough Draft)*
Write your first draft of the paragraph. Do not worry about perfect grammar, spelling, punctuation, or capitalization for this draft. Make sure you write this first draft using the ideas on the chart/outline (page 58). Be sure to include the following in your rough draft:

• A title
• A topic sentence at the beginning of the paragraph
• Enough support with descriptive details
• Enough details to paint a vivid picture (at least five or six sentences)
• Words from as many boxes on the chart (page 54) as possible
• At least three vocabulary words from this lesson

After You Write

Check Your Work

After you finish writing the first draft, read your paragraph again. Check your work for the following. Do this before you show it to anyone else.

☐ This paragraph discusses one of the following:

  • my (or my friend's or my relative's) body art/decoration

  • body art or decoration in my culture

  • a specific ceremony or celebration that includes body art/decoration

☐ This paragraph has a title.

☐ This paragraph has a topic sentence.

☐ This paragraph has at least five or six sentences of description.

☐ All of the descriptive sentences relate to the topic sentence,

☐ I used as many words and expressions from the chart in Step One as possible.

☐ I used three vocabulary words from this lesson in the paragraph.

☐ I used several sentence patterns, such as subject + verb, subject + verb + object, and linking verbs with adjectives, nouns, and prepositions.

☐ I checked my sentences for fragments (missing subjects or verbs).

This paragraph has correct paragraph form as follows:

☐ The title is centered above the paragraph.

☐ The title has correct capitalization.

☐ My title does not end in a period.

☐ I indented the first sentence of the paragraph.

☐ I have correct margins on the left and right.

☐ I did not put punctuation (period, comma, question mark) at the beginning of a new line.

☐ I double-spaced (skipped a space after every line).

☐ All of my sentences follow one another. (I did not go to the next line with a new sentence.)

■ **Step Five: Getting Feedback about the First Draft**

Show someone your first draft of the paragraph. Your teacher will decide the type of feedback you will receive for the first draft. It may be with a partner or from the teacher or both ways. For review with a partner, use the sheet on page 192 in the Appendix.

■ **Step Six: Making Changes**

After you receive feedback, make some changes. First, decide if you want to change your topic sentence. Then decide if you want to change your supporting sentences by adding new ones or taking out some. Make sure you have a vivid description, and the reader can clearly see what you are describing. After you make these changes, look at all the grammar, punctuation, spelling, and capitalization. Make any necessary changes in these things as well.

■ **Step Seven: The Final Draft**

Type your final draft on a computer. Try to make this paragraph as perfect as you can.

Organizing Your Thoughts for Writing

TITLE: _____

TOPIC SENTENCE

Descriptive detail	Descriptive detail
Support for detail	Support for detail
Descriptive detail	Descriptive detail
Support for detail	Support for detail

SUPPORT

SUPPORT

Mexican Americans

Content Area: History

Reading: Early History of Mexican Americans

Short Readings: Migration North
The 1920s and 1930s
The Bracero Program
Twentieth Century Movements Toward Reform
Dolores Huerta
Cesar Chavez

Sentence Writing Focus: Combining Sentences with Coordinating
Conjunctions

Editing Focus: Run-ons/Comma Splices

Writing Focus: Paragraphs (Facts/Biographies) Concluding Sentences

PART 1   UNIT PREVIEW

■ Preview Activity: Discussion Questions and Maps

*A. How much do you know about the history of Mexican Americans? Answer the following questions. Write **T** for "True" or **F** for "False."*

_____ 1. The land that is now Texas, California, Arizona, New Mexico, and parts of Colorado, Nevada, and Utah was at one time part of Mexico.

_____ 2. Mexican farm workers came to the United States to work only within the last 50 to 60 years.

_____ 3. There were very few Mexican Americans in the United States before 1920.

_____ 4. In the past, some industries and the United States Government asked Mexicans to come to the United States to work.

B. Below and on page 61 you will find a timeline and three numbered maps of Mexico and parts of the United States. Write the number of each map in the correct time frame on the timeline.

1519   1600   1700   1800   1900   1920

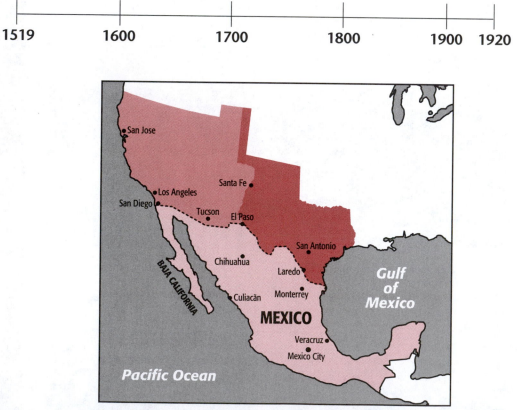

1. Independent Mexico's loss of land to U.S.

2. U.S. states formed by Mexico's land loss

3. Colonial New Spain

Share your answers with a partner and/or the class.

Quickwrite/Freewrite

Write for five minutes about the following topic. Do not worry about grammar, spelling, or punctuation. Just write what comes to your mind about the topic.

- Where does your family originally come from? In the past did your family move to new places, or did they stay in one area, city, or town? When did you or your family come to the place you are living now?

PART 2   READING AND VOCABULARY

Early History of Mexican Americans

The United States is a country of **immigrants** from different countries and cultures. Many people came here on long **journeys** across oceans, but Mexican Americans did not take such trips. Some Mexican Americans **descend** from original Indian cultures or a mixture of those cultures with the first Spanish **settlers.** Most of today's Mexican Americans have **ancestors** who arrived more recently, or they are new immigrants themselves. We can divide the history of Mexican Americans, or Chicanos as they are often called, into several time periods.

The earliest known **inhabitants** of North America, the Native Americans or Indians, lived here for thousands of years before the first Europeans arrived. The Spanish **conquistadores** first came to Mexico in 1519. During the following **century** they **colonized** a large area of land, including present-day Mexico and the southwestern United States (see Map 3 on p. 61). They called this area New Spain and **imposed** a new way of life on the Native Americans already living there. Soon there was a **blending** of these two worlds to create a mestizo (mixed) culture.

In 1810, almost three hundred years after the arrival of the Spaniards, Mexicans began to **rebel** against Spanish rule. In 1821 Mexico became independent, but over the next 27 years the central government in Mexico City had trouble controlling the country's northern areas. First, Texas became independent from Mexico in 1836, and ten years later there was a war between Mexico and the United States. As a result of that war, in 1848 Mexico lost much of its **territory**, and a large part of its northern lands became a part of the United States (see Map 2 on p. 61). At that time approximately 80,000 Mexicans were living north of the Rio Grande River. Under the **treaty** of Guadeloupe Hidalgo, many of them became the first Mexican American **citizens** in the United States because of the new U.S./Mexican border.

During the next period, from the end of the Mexican American War until the end of the nineteenth century, the southwestern part of the United States **underwent** changes as it became part of a new country. People from other parts of the United States as well as new types of businesses moved into the area. Railroads, **mines, lumber, livestock,** and **agriculture** all began to bring the southwest into the larger **economy** of the United States. Mexican Americans found jobs, mostly in railroads, agriculture, and mining, but they often received low **wages** for their work and became second-class citizens.

Comprehension Check

*A. **Main Idea**   Circle the letter of your answer for each of the following.*

1. This reading is mainly about

   a. the history of Mexican Americans from thousands of years ago to today.

   b. the history of some of the first Mexican Americans through the 1800s.

   c. the history of both Mexicans and Native Americans in the U.S. southwest.

*B. **Details***
Below you will find a list of details about each of the three time periods discussed in this reading. Write the numbers of the detailed information on the correct point on the timeline. Follow the example.

```
 |──────────────┼──────────────┼──────1.──────|
early history      1809           1847          1890s
```

1. Businesses, such as agriculture and lumber came to the southwestern part of the United States.

2. Native Americans lived in the area.

3. Mexicans living north of the Rio Grande became U.S. citizens.

4. Mexico gained independence from Spain.

5. A mestizo culture developed in New Spain.

6. Southwestern U.S. changed because of new borders.

7. Texas became independent from Mexico.

8. Mexico lost much of its land to the United States.

Decide if the following statements are true or false based on the reading.
*Write **T** for "True" or **F** for "False."*

_____ 1. Most people in the United States today came from Mexico.

_____ 2. Some Mexican Americans come from families with very old histories in Mexico and the United States.

_____ 3. The Spanish arrived in the area that is now Mexico soon after the Native Americans came there.

_____ 4. Mexico's name as a Spanish colony was New Spain.

_____ 5. The mestizo culture is another name for Native Americans.

_____ 6. Texas became independent from Mexico before Mexico became independent from Spain.

_____ 7. After the Mexican American War, a large part of Mexico became the United States.

_____ 8. Mexicans living north of the Rio Grande River had to immediately return to Mexico after the Mexican American War.

_____ 9. Mexican Americans found jobs in different businesses in the southwest during the 1800s.

_____ 10. Mexican Americans working in the southwestern part of the United States made a lot of money and had easy lives.

Vocabulary Study

A. *Below you will find an underlined vocabulary word from the reading in each sentence and four definitions or synonyms after that sentence. Circle the two choices that have the same meaning as the vocabulary word. Follow the example.*

1. There was a <u>blending</u> of different people and cultures in the south-western United States.

   a. mixture   b. combination

   c. separation   d. disagreement

2. When people move from one country to another over large areas of land, it can be a difficult <u>journey.</u>

   a. kind of transportation   b. season

   c. trip   d. passage from one place to another

3. Sometimes governments <u>impose</u> a tax or other kind of extra fee on goods, such as gasoline.

   a. force   b. ask for

   c. remove   d. require

4. When people are living in terrible conditions, they may <u>rebel</u> to try to get a new government.

   a. accept   b. resist

   c. go against   d. vote

5. Mexican Americans often received lower <u>wages</u> than other groups of workers on the same kinds of job.

   a. food   b. salary

   c. education   d. earnings

6. When two countries stop fighting or end a disagreement, they often make a <u>treaty.</u>

   a. big party   b. holiday

   c. agreement   d. formal contract in writing

B. *Choose a definition/synonym from the following list for each of the under-lined vocabulary words in the sentences. Write the letter of the answer on the line next to the sentence. The first one has been done as an example.*

a. come from   b. geographic areas   c. experience

~~d. period of 100 years~~   e. make an area subject to another country

___d___ 1. In the past very few people lived for a full <u>century</u>, but today it is becoming more common.

_____ 2. Some people <u>descend</u> from families who came to California from Mexico over 100 years ago.

_____ 3. During the 1600s and 1700s several European countries <u>colonized</u> areas in Africa, Asia, and South America.

_____ 4. Sometimes two countries argue and fight wars over <u>territory</u> they both want.

_____ 5. When people move from one place to a very different place, they may <u>undergo</u> some difficulties.

C. *Each of the words below comes from the reading and is a kind of person. For each word write the letter of the meanings that follow. Some words may have more than one meaning from the list.*

____ immigrant   ____ inhabitant   ____ settler
____ conquistador   ____ citizen   ____ ancestor

Meanings

a. person who comes to stay in a new place

b. newcomer

c. legal resident

d. resident

e. person who moves from one place to another to live permanently

f. conqueror or soldier

g. family before grandparents

D. *Match the following types of businesses or industries mentioned in the reading with their meanings.*

A	B
1. agriculture	a. farm animals
2. lumber	b. trains
3. livestock	c. place where people take minerals and ores from the earth
4. mining	d. farming
5. railroads	e. wood (ready for construction)

Discussion/Writing

Your teacher will tell you to answer these questions in writing or through discussion.

1. What do you know about the history of the place you came from or are now living in? Who were the first people to live there?

2. What blending of cultures can you find in the place where you came from or are now living? Describe these cultures.

PART 3   WRITING SENTENCES—SENTENCE COMBINING WITH COORDINATING CONJUNCTIONS

Read the paragraph about the more recent history of Mexican Americans and answer the questions that follow.

Reading

Migration North

[1]By the 1890s the population of Mexican Americans was increasing, but many more Mexicans left their homeland after 1900 looking for work and a better life. [2]At that time people could enter the United States without passports, so many new immigrants crossed the border north from Mexico. [3]In 1910 a civil war began in Mexico, and thousands of people escaped to the United States. [4]Some people came with their entire families, but some men chose to come alone. [5]In the United States those men could often find jobs on the railroads, or they could work in mining. [6]Many families found work in agriculture, such as picking cotton or various fruits and vegetables. [7]Most of these new immigrants worked as manual laborers, but they did not have a chance to learn the more skilled jobs. [8]Also, their living and working conditions were often very difficult. [9]The railroad workers often lived in boxcars or other poor housing along the railroad tracks. [10]The families of agricultural laborers lived in tents or wooden shacks with one or two rooms for the whole family. [11]Many of these people became migrant farm workers, so they traveled north each summer and fall to find work in the fields. [12]In general, the many Mexican immigrants of the early 1900s were able to escape the harsh conditions of their homeland, but they had little opportunity to become part of the main culture of their new home.

Questions

1. How many subject-verb combinations do you see in sentence 3 of the reading above? Underline each of those. What word is putting those sentences together? Circle that word.

2. Follow the same instructions in question 1 for sentence 2, sentence 4, and sentence 5 in the reading.

3. On the lines below write each word you circled for questions 1 and 2. Write one word on each line.

_____   _____   _____   _____

Explanation: Combining Sentences with Coordinating Conjunctions

Sentence-Combining Focus

Coordinating Conjunctions (and/but/so/or)

1. Review of Units One and Two—There are several patterns for writing simple sentences in English. In addition, every simple sentence must have at least a subject and a verb.

   a. After 1900 many *immigrants* in the U.S. *were from Mexico*.

       subject   linking   prepositional phrase
                        verb

   b. Many *immigrants crossed* the *border* north from Mexico.

       subject   verb   object

   c. Their living and working *conditions were* often very *difficult*.

           subject   linking verb   adjective

   d. Many of these *people became* migrant farm *workers*.

       subject   linking verb   noun (identification)

   e. The *families* of agricultural laborers *lived* in tents or wooden shacks.

       subject   verb   (no object)

2. A sentence with one subject-verb combination is also called a *clause*. Speakers and writers do not use only simple sentences (clauses) when they communicate. They often put sentences (clauses) together or combine them to make bigger sentences. There are several ways to combine sentences/clauses. In each case you add a signal or extra piece to the sentence. This signal or *connector* shows you are combining more than one idea.

3. In this lesson you will learn about one group of signals called *coordinating conjunctions*. Each coordinating conjunction has a specific meaning and shows a relationship between the second clause and the first as follows:

   a. Conjunction showing more information: *and*

      In 1910 a civil war began in Mexico,
      clause #1
      and _thousands of people escaped to the United States_.
            clause #2 (more information)

b. Conjunction showing contrast: *but*

   By the 1890s the population of Mexican Americans was increasing,
   clause #1

   but *many more Mexicans left their homeland after 1900.*
      clause #2 (contrast)

c. Conjunction showing result/conclusion: *so*

   At that time people could enter the United States without passports,
   clause #1

   so *many new immigrants crossed the border north from Mexico.*
      clause #2 (result)

d. Conjunction showing choice/two possibilities: *or*

   In the United States those men could often find jobs on the railroads,
   clause #1

   or *they could work in mining.*
      clause #2 (choice)

4. You will usually find these conjunctions in the middle of a sentence between the two clauses. When you use these words, follow this pattern:

   _____,   ☐   _____
         clause #1   conjunction   clause #2

NOTE: Sometimes you will find these words at the beginning of a sentence. This is acceptable in some situations (usually informal English) but not in formal academic English. When you are writing for school or business, try not to begin your sentences with these words.

5. Punctuation and capitalization with conjunctions

   a. Place the comma <u>before</u> the conjunction at the end of the first clause.

   INCORRECT: In 1910 a civil war began in Mexico and, thousands of people escaped to the United States.

   CORRECT: In 1910 a civil war began in Mexico, **and** thousands of people escaped to the United States.

   b. Only the first word of the sentence should have a capital letter. Do not use a capital letter in the middle of the sentence.

   INCORRECT: A terrible civil war began in Mexico, and Thousands of people escaped to the United States.

   CORRECT: A terrible civil war began in Mexico, **and t**housands of people escaped to the United States.

6. Be careful! Not every *and*, *but*, *so*, and *or* is a conjunction putting sentences together. Look carefully at the following examples:

The railroad workers often lived in **boxcars *or* other poor**

      subject   verb   noun

housing along the railroad tracks.

  noun

Many families found work in agriculture, such as picking

     subject   verb

cotton *or* various fruits *and* vegetables.

  noun   noun   noun

In these examples the words *or* and *and* are not combining sentences. There is only one subject-verb combination in each of these sentences. Notice there are no commas with *and* and *or*. This is because they are connecting two nouns and not two clauses.

NOTE: Sometimes you may want to make a list of more than two nouns. In these cases use a comma after each noun and use the word *and* between the last two nouns on the list.

Workers picked cotton and strawberries. (no comma—two items)
Workers picked cotton, strawberries, and tomatoes in the fields.
Workers picked cotton, strawberries, tomatoes, and corn in the fields.

7. **Important—Errors to Avoid**

a. **Run-on sentences**   Do not combine sentences without a signal or connector, such as a coordinating conjunction. Doing this will make a *run-on* sentence. A run-on sentence is not acceptable in written English.

Editing Focus

Run-ons,
Comma Splices

INCORRECT: run on
Some people came with their entire families some men chose to come alone.
    subject verb   subject verb

CORRECT: Some people came with their entire families, **but** some
                men chose to come alone.

b. **Comma splices**   Do not connect clauses with just a comma and no other signal. A comma by itself is not an acceptable signal or connector. Putting a comma by itself between two clauses will make a *comma splice*. A comma splice is not acceptable in written English.

INCORRECT: comma splice
Some people came with their entire families, some men chose to come alone.
    subject verb   subject verb

CORRECT: Some people came with their entire families, **but** some
                men chose to come alone.

NOTE: You can also correct run-ons and comma splices by making separate sentences without a conjunction.

> Some people came with their entire families. Some men chose to come alone.

This is grammatically correct, and sometimes you may want to write two simple sentences. However, it's a good idea to try to have variety in your sentences as well. This means sometimes you should write simple sentences, and other times your sentences should be longer using connectors, such as coordinating conjunctions.

Practice: Sentence Combining—Using Coordinating Conjunctions

A. **Identifying Clauses and Coordinating Conjunctions** *Underline each clause and circle each coordinating conjunction in the sentences below. (Each sentence has two clauses and one conjunction.) Follow the example in sentence 1.*

non-Spanish whites

1. <u>After the Mexican-American War Anglos built towns and businesses,</u> (and) <u>the economy of the southwestern United States grew.</u>

2. The nineteenth century was a difficult period for many Mexicans, but it was a time of economic growth for the southwestern United States.

3. Starting in 1849 new mines opened in several parts of the United States, so miners and settlers came to these areas to work.

4. Miners could work in the many mines of Arizona and New Mexico, or they could find jobs in the salt mines of Texas.

B. Matching Clauses *Match the clause in column A with the coordinating conjunction and clause that best fits in column B. Use each answer only one time.*

A	B
_____ 1. For many years Chinese immigrants worked on the railroads,	a. and small communities called *colonias* developed.
_____ 2. The Chinese Exclusion Act limited the number of new Chinese immigrants in the U.S.,	b. but in 1882 a new law limited their immigration into the United States.
_____ 3. In the 1880s many Mexicans found work in the U.S. making new railroad lines,	c. so many Mexicans began to work on the railroads.
_____ 4. Often these Mexican workers lived near their jobs on the railroad lines,	d. or they repaired and maintained existing lines.

C. ***Combining Sentences***   *Combine the two sentences next to each number using the coordinating conjunction given in parentheses. Be sure to use correct punctuation. Follow the example.*

1. (but) There were many opportunities for Mexican people to work in the fields. The pay was low for difficult work.

   <u>There were many opportunities for Mexican people to work in the fields, but the pay was low for difficult work.</u>

2. (so) Farmers needed hand laborers to work in their fields.
   They encouraged the migration of Mexicans to come north.

   _____

   _____

3. (but) There was much work in the fields in summer or fall.
   There was often little or no work at all in the winter.

   _____

   _____

4. (or) Farm workers had to earn enough money in summer and fall to use in the winter months.
   They had to find other kinds of work to support their families and themselves.

   _____

   _____

5. (and) Sometimes growers had work all year round.
   They wanted Mexican Americans to work on their farms permanently.

   _____

   _____

6. (so) Other farmers needed workers only during certain seasons.
   Those workers traveled from one field to another as migrant workers.

   _____

   _____

D. ***Choosing the Correct Conjunction to Combine Sentences***   *Choose the coordinating conjunction in parentheses that makes the best relationship between the two sentences. Then write one sentence by combining the two using the conjunction you chose. Be sure to add correct punctuation. Follow the example.*

1. (so/but) Until the beginning of the twentieth century, there were no formal border controls between Mexico and the United States. People crossed easily from one country to the other.

   <u>Until the beginning of the 20th century, there were no formal border controls between Mexico and the United Sates, so people crossed easily from one country to the other.</u>

2. (or/and) Different groups of Mexicans have migrated to the US since 1900. They came in several groups or "waves."

_____

_____

3. (so/but) The first wave began at the turn of the century. It was not the biggest group.

_____

_____

4. (or/but) Before 1910 Mexicans came because of economic problems. They were unhappy with the political situation before their country's civil war.

_____

_____

5. (but/so) Many refugees from the Mexican civil war were uneducated and poor. They had to accept low-paying jobs to survive.

_____

_____

6. (and/or) Some others came from Mexico with money of their own. They started their own businesses.

_____

_____

 *E. **Completing Sentences on Your Own**   Review the reading in Part 2 (page 62). Complete the following sentences with information you learned from this reading. Use the coordinating conjunction given in parentheses and write a complete clause after the conjunction. Be sure to use your own words in your answers and include correct punctuation. Follow the example.*

1. (and) The Spanish Conquistadores came to Mexico in 1519, <u>and they created a colony called New Spain.</u>

2. (but) Native Americans were already living in the area called New Spain

_____

3. (so) In the early 1800s the Mexicans rebelled against Spanish rule

_____

4. (and) There was a war between Mexico and the United States in 1848

_____

5. (or) Under the treaty of Guadeloupe Hidalgo, Mexicans north of the Rio Grande River could go back to Mexico

_____

6. (so) The southwestern part of the United States became part of the U.S. after the war with Mexico

_____

7. (or) In the late nineteenth century, Mexicans in the United States could work on the railroads

_____

8. (but) Mexican Americans often found work in the United States

_____

F. *Finding Sentence Problems*

1. *Run-ons*   Each sentence below is a run-on. Find each problem and show how to change it into two simple sentences. Then write the sentence correctly using the coordinating conjunction on the lines given. Be sure to use correct punctuation. Follow the example.

Editing Focus
Run-ons;
Comma Splices

> EXAMPLE: A large wave of Mexican immigrants started in 1914 at the beginning of World War 1. it continued through the 1920s.
>
> (and) A large wave of Mexican immigrants started in 1914 at the beginning of World War I, and it continued through the 1920s.

a. Most of these people were running away from poverty in Mexico some left for religious reasons.

(but)

b. Growing industries in the southwestern U.S. had jobs available they welcomed these new workers.

(so)

c. Many of the over one million immigrants in this wave were *peasant* farmers they were small tradesmen/craftsmen.   poor

(or)

d. These new immigrants reminded the settled Mexican Americans of their Mexican culture in the U.S. they helped increase awareness of their cultural roots.

(and)

e. This was a larger wave of people than the one before many present-day Mexican American communities developed from this group.

(so)

2. *Comma Splices*   Each sentence below is a comma splice. Find each problem and show how to change it into two simple sentences. Then write the sentence correctly using the coordinating conjunction on the lines given. Be sure to use correct punctuation. Follow the example.

EXAMPLE:

World War I took place between 1914 and 1918.^ ~~d~~during this time the Mexican American community began to leave the three usual fields of employment.

(and) _World War I took place between 1914 and 1918, and during this time_ _the Mexican American community began to leave the three usual fields of_ _employment._

a. Many men from the US were fighting in the war, there was a need for factory workers.

(so)

b. Mexican Americans could stay in the southwest areas of the U.S., they could travel north to look for work.

(or)

c. Also, wages in the southwest agricultural jobs were low, many people went north to find higher paying jobs.

(so)

d. By the end of the 1920s, some Mexican Americans were still working in agriculture, many found jobs as mechanics, machinists, and painters.

(but)

e. Some were working in meatpacking plants, others found jobs in the steel mills of Ohio and Pennsylvania.

(and)

3. *Run-ons and Comma Splices*   The following paragraph has 3 run-ons and 3 commas splices. Find the mistakes and show how to correct each one using a coordinating conjunction. Be sure to use each of the four conjunctions from this lesson (*and, but, so, or*) at least once in your corrections.

The 1920s and 1930s

The United States government welcomed Mexican immigrant workers in the 1920s, but it sent many people back to Mexico in the 1930s. In the 1920s the United States economy was good, there was a growing demand for unskilled labor. Immigration laws limited Asian and Eastern European immigrants they did not limit Mexicans. Between 1920 and 1929 about 600,000 Mexicans entered the United States on permanent visas as legal residents. These newcomers often found jobs in agriculture, they found jobs in manufacturing. In addition, many *undocumented* workers came across the border the United States established a Border Patrol to control this kind of immigration in 1924. During the 1930s there was a Depression in the United States many people needed work. Under a program called "repatriation" police and government agents sent many Mexicans back to Mexico. During the early 1930s they deported hundreds of thousands of Mexican Americans, not all of those people were undocumented immigrants. This included United States citizens of Mexican descent as well as legal residents. This time in the twentieth century was one example of the "push-pull pattern" of Mexican immigrant labor in the United States.

without
official papers

Discussion/Writing

Your teacher will tell you to answer these questions in writing or through discussion.

1. Do you live in an area of farms and open land or a city with more factories and businesses? Describe the life of most people who live in this area.

2. What kind of economy does the area you are now living in have? In other words, what kinds of businesses and industries can you find there? What kind(s) of jobs do many people have in the area where you are now living?

PART 4   WRITING PARAGRAPHS (FACTS/ BIOGRAPHIES)/CONCLUDING SENTENCES

Read the following paragraph about the Bracero Program and then answer the questions that follow.

The Bracero Program

Between 1942 and 1964 the Bracero Program brought another large wave of Mexican workers to the United States to provide much needed labor. After the United States entered World War II, a labor shortage developed. Then the United States and Mexico made an agreement to bring temporary contract workers, or *braceros,* into the United States to work for a season and return to Mexico. Working conditions were difficult, but the braceros contributed to the war effort by helping to produce food in the fields and transport soldiers and supplies on the railroads. During the second phase of this program from 1948 to 1951 farmers and businesses made their own contracts for workers. However, the United States and Mexico made another agreement during this time. In 1949 they agreed to legalize more than 87,000 undocumented workers as braceros. In the 1950s the Mexican government again wanted a formal agreement, and the largest group of braceros came during this third phase. These workers continued to face dangerous working conditions and mistreatment through the years until the program ended in 1964. In conclusion, the Bracero Program was an example of a familiar pattern of bringing large numbers of Mexican laborers to help U.S. businesses and industries.

Paragraph Discussion

1. Does this paragraph follow correct paragraph format? Does it have all of the following?

   ___ a title centered above the paragraph

   ___ correct capitalization of the title

   ___ indenting of the first sentence

   ___ each sentence following the one before

   ___ correct left and right margins

   ___ a capital letter at the beginning of each new sentence

   ___ end punctuation for each sentence

2. Which sentence in this paragraph is the topic sentence? What is the topic and what is the controlling idea of this sentence?

3. How many supporting sentences are in this paragraph?

4. What kind of information do the supporting sentences give?

5. What information does the last sentence give? What is the purpose of the last sentence?

Paragraph Organization

Writing Focus

Paragraph Organization: Facts and Concluding Sentences

Supporting Sentences/Using Facts: Sometimes writers use facts in their supporting sentences to provide specific information about a subject. A fact is something that is always true. You can prove a fact because it does not change. For example, the Bracero Program began in 1942 and ended in 1964. These are facts and those dates will not change. Sometimes writers may use dates, names, and numbers to add facts to their writing.

Look back at the paragraph about the Bracero Program (page 76) and circle all of the names, dates, and numbers. What do you notice about capital letters in the words you circled?

Paragraph Organization Review: In previous units you learned about writing paragraphs by starting with a topic sentence and following it with several sentences of support. The topic sentence is a general statement, and it gives the main idea of the paragraph. The supporting sentences provide details about that main idea. These details may include examples, descriptions, and facts.

Concluding Sentences: At the end of a paragraph you will often find a concluding sentence. A concluding sentence:

a. is the last sentence in the paragraph.

b. is a general statement.

c. tells the reader that the paragraph is finished.

There are different ways to write a concluding sentence. One way is to restate the main idea of the paragraph or the topic sentence.

Restating the Topic Sentence/Main Idea of the Paragraph: A concluding sentence can remind the reader of the main idea of the paragraph. It may be similar to the topic sentence, but the two sentences should not be exactly the same. A concluding sentence may contain some of the same words as the topic sentence, but these should be only a few of the most important or *key* words. This kind of concluding sentence should use different words that mean the same as the ideas in the topic sentence.

EXAMPLE TOPIC SENTENCE:
During World War I between 1914 and 1918, the Mexican American community began to find work in different areas of employment.

Which one of the following sentences is a good concluding sentence that restates the main idea?

a. In conclusion, during World War I between 1914 to 1918, the Mexican American community began to find work outside their three usual areas of employment.

b. In conclusion, Mexican Americans were successful in finding jobs outside their usual areas of employment during the World War I years.

c. In conclusion, Mexican workers found work in the United States during World War I.

Answer: The best concluding sentence for the topic sentence is b. Notice that some of the words are the same in the topic sentence, but some ideas are the same in different words.

Same words: World War I, Mexican American, areas of employment

Same ideas using different words:

during World War I between 1914 and 1918	during the World War I years
the Mexican American community	Mexican Americans
began to find work	were successful in finding jobs
in different areas of employment	outside their usual areas of employment

Sentence *a.* is almost exactly the same as the topic sentence, so it is not a good concluding sentence. Too many of the words are the same in both sentences.

Sentence *c.* does not give the main idea of the paragraph. The paragraph is about how Mexican Americans found different kinds of jobs, and sentence c. states only that they found jobs in general.

Practice: Paragraph Organization—Topic Sentences, Supporting Facts, and Conclusions

Paragraph Analysis

A. Look back at the paragraph about the Bracero Program (page 76) and complete the following activities.

1. Fill in the chart below with the title and then the topic sentence on the lines given. Write the topic sentence on the roof line of the chart exactly as it appears in the paragraph.

2. Fill in the details in the boxes under the topic sentence, including facts. Do not write whole sentences from the paragraph. Just write some words. Follow the example in the first box.

3. Write the concluding sentence on the line given for the floor of the house. Write the whole sentence exactly as it appears in the original paragraph.

TITLE: _____

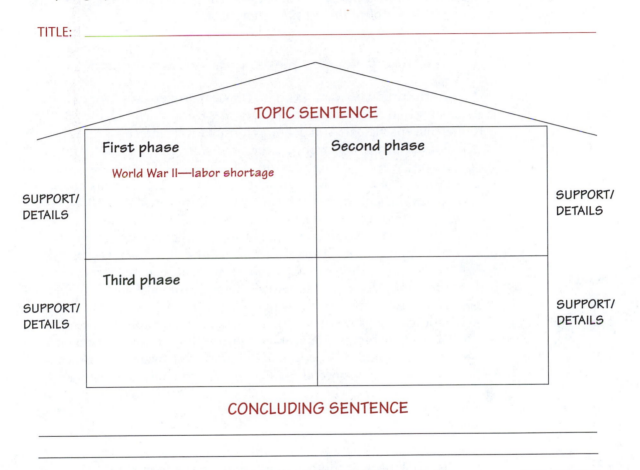

TOPIC SENTENCE

First phase

World War II—labor shortage

Second phase

SUPPORT/ DETAILS

Third phase

SUPPORT/ DETAILS

SUPPORT/ DETAILS

SUPPORT/ DETAILS

CONCLUDING SENTENCE

_____
_____
_____

4. Now look at the topic sentence and concluding sentence on the chart. Is this concluding sentence a restatement of the topic sentence? What words are the same? Write them below:

_____

What ideas are the same with different words? Write them on the line below.

_____

Remember: A concluding sentence does NOT

a. come at the beginning or middle of the paragraph.

b. discuss or explain a detail from the paragraph.

c. add any new details to the paragraph.

d. use too many of the same words as the topic sentence. (It should not look exactly like the topic sentence.)

Paragraph Analysis

B. Read the following paragraph about Mexican Americans in the twentieth century. Then complete the activities that follow.

Twentieth Century Movements Toward Reform

During the twentieth century Mexican Americans worked to establish social and economic changes in several ways. In the early 1900s they participated in labor reform movements by protesting their difficult living and working conditions. In the 1920s California workers organized the Confederation of Unions of Mexican Workers (CUMW) and led a *strike* against farmers in 1928. Organizations, such as the League of United Latin American Citizens (LULAC—formed in 1929) worked to educate the people about social, political, and economic issues and fought for more equal education and job opportunities. During the 1950s and '60s a movement of ethnic pride, called the Chicano Movement, began. During that time another organization, called the National Farm Workers Association (NFW) also led strikes and protests to help farm workers improve their conditions. In the following decades political organizations worked more and more toward organizing the Mexican American community. For example, Mexican Americans won several political offices, such as governors and mayors of large cities.

work stoppage

1. Look back at the paragraph and do the following:

a. Underline the topic sentence.

b. Circle the years given in the paragraph.

c. Underline all the names in the paragraph.

2. Circle the letter of the concluding sentence that best restates the topic sentence/main idea of the paragraph. Be prepared to explain your answer.

a. In conclusion, Mexican Americans were able to organize and make some economic and social changes during the 1900s.

  b. In conclusion, during the 1900s Mexican Americans worked to make social and economic changes in several ways.

  c. In conclusion, Mexican Americans organized a Chicano Movement in the 1970s and 1980s.

Paragraph Organization

C. Look at the following information for a paragraph about the "push-pull" pattern of Mexican worker migration to the United States. Read the title and topic sentence. Decide if all the details fit for this paragraph. Then choose the best conclusion.

Title: The "Push-Pull" Pattern of Migration North

Topic Sentence: The story of Mexican migration to the north during the past 125 years involves a pattern of encouragement to enter the work force in the United States as well as discouragement and deportation back to Mexico.

Details:

1. 1880s—Chinese exclusion—Mexicans encouraged to work on the railroads to reduce labor shortages

2. early 1900s—laws about immigration affect people from many countries (Asia/Europe). These laws do not affect Mexicans, so they continue to enter the United States to work.

3. 1920s—large numbers of Mexicans come to the United States to supply labor

4. 1930s—repatriation program—many Mexican American workers deported back to Mexico

5. 1940s and '50s—Bracero Program—Mexicans brought into the United States as seasonal workers and many stay as immigrants

6. 1954—"Operation Wetback"—United States immigration arrests and deports almost 4 million workers of Mexican descent

Conclusion: Circle the letter of the best concluding sentence for this paragraph.

  a. Mexican workers came to the United States in the Bracero Program because of a labor shortage, but many had to leave in the 1960s.

  b. Many Mexican workers came to the United States to work in agricultural jobs during the nineteenth and twentieth centuries.

  c. In conclusion, the "push-pull" pattern of encouragement and discouragement of Mexican immigrant labor in the United States occurred several times in the past 125 years.

BIOGRAPHIES

Read the following about a well-known Chicana (Mexican-American woman) and answer the questions that follow it.

Dolores Huerta

Dolores Huerta is a tireless and powerful Mexican-American labor leader and social activist. She was born in 1930 in the small mining town of Dawson, New Mexico, and she grew up in the farming town of Stockton, California. She became a teacher, but then she decided to help the poor families of her students by becoming active in the community. In 1955 she helped start a chapter of a Mexican-American self-help group called Community Service Organization (CSO). She registered people to vote, organized citizenship classes for immigrants, and pressured local governments to make improvements in *barrios*. While doing this work, she also recognized the needs of farm workers, and in 1960 she started the Agricultural Workers Association. At age 25, she worked to change laws to help farm workers and other immigrants in California. In 1962 she worked in Washington, DC to end the Bracero Program. Then she and another activist (Cesar Chavez) began a new organization, called the National Farm Workers Association. For many years Dolores worked with Chavez to organize nonviolent protests and boycotts to gain contracts for better wages and working conditions for farm workers. Today she continues to work long hours as a community organizer in her position as President of the Dolores Huerta Foundation. Dolores Huerta spent much of her life working for justice and equality for immigrant workers in all industries, and she continues to do so today.

Spanish speaking neighborhoods

Paragraph Discussion—Biography

Often when studying history, you will find information about people's lives. These stories are called *biographies*. A biography usually gives factual information, including important names, dates, and places as well as the person's accomplishments or achievements. Accomplishments or achievements are a person's successes or things that a person was able to complete. When someone writes his or her own biography, we call it an *autobiography*.

Look back at the paragraph about Dolores Huerta and circle all the dates and names of people, places, and organizations you can find. Then put a line under each accomplishment or achievement discussed in the paragraph.

Practice: Paragraph Organization

A. Read the following information about another famous Mexican American, Henry Cisneros. Then answer the questions that follow.

Title: Henry Cisneros

Topic Sentence: One of the most successful and well-known Mexican-American politicians and community leaders today is Henry Cisneros.

Support/Details:

1. born in San Antonio, Texas in 1947

2. has family stories about descending from people from Spain and the mestizos.

3. received several college degrees, including a BA and MA in regional planning and an MPA and PhD in public administration

4. 1975—elected to the City Council of San Antonio

5. 1975—two other Mexican Americans elected to office as governors of Arizona and New Mexico

6. 1981—became the first Mexican-American mayor of a major US city (San Antonio, Texas)

7. reelected mayor in 1983 and 1985

8. 1985—elected president of the National League of Cities

9. left government to chair his own company (Cisneros Asset Management) working with nonprofit organizations

10. 1993–1997—served as Secretary of the Department of Housing and Urban Development under President Clinton

Questions

1. Which two of the support/details above do not belong in a biography of Henry Cisneros's life? Cross out those two details.

2. Which of the following is the best concluding sentence for the paragraph about Henry Cisneros? Circle the letter of your answer.

   a. Henry Cisneros held an important government position under President Clinton in the 1990s.

   b. Henry Cisneros is one example of a successful Mexican-American public figure and community leader.

   c. Henry Cisneros is well-known because he was the first Mexican-American mayor of a major U.S. city.

Writing a Conclusion:

B. The following biography about Cesar Chavez needs a conclusion. Read the paragraph and write a conclusion on the lines given.

Cesar Chavez

not eating

protesting by not eating
refusal to buy or
do business with

One heroic Chicano leader, Cesar Chavez, spent much of his life helping improve the lives of agricultural workers. Born in 1927, Chavez worked with his family in the fields and vineyards of California as early as the age of ten. They traveled to so many different fields that Cesar attended more than 30 different schools as a child, and he never went beyond the eighth grade. In the 1950s he worked for the Community Service Organization (CSO), and he began to organize the poorly paid and poorly treated grape pickers in his area of California. He continued this work throughout California, and ten years later he started the National Farm Workers Association. This group later became the United Farm Workers of America (UFW). He led thousands of farm workers on strikes, *fasts*, and marches in order to help them bargain as a group for better wages. In 1965 he led a 300 mile march from central California to Sacramento and went on a *hunger strike* for 25 days. Three years later he led a national *boycott* of California table grapes. After five years the grape growers agreed to the changes, and the strike was over. During the 1970s and 1980s Chavez continued to help farm workers through peaceful means, such as protests, boycotts, and fasting. He died at the age of 66 from his life of difficult conditions and fasting.

_____

_____

Discussion/Writing

Your teacher will tell you to answer these questions in writing or through discussion.

1. What are some important dates and places in your life or the life of someone in your family? Why are these dates and places important?

2. Name one famous person from your native culture. What do you know about this person's life? Discuss some of his/her accomplishments or achievements.

Writing Assignment

Picking the Topic

Choose one of the following topics and write a paragraph about it. Be sure to include a topic sentence, facts and examples in your support, and a concluding sentence.

1. Write a paragraph about your family history. Write about your parents, grandparents, and any other ancestors you may know about. Be sure to use facts, such as dates, numbers, and places. Think about the following when you write the paragraph:

   • Where does your family come from?

   • When did they move to the place you are now living?

   • What kind of jobs or work did/do the people in your family have?

2. Write a biography about yourself (an autobiography) or one person in your family in one paragraph. You should write about someone you know well. Be sure to use facts, such as dates, names, and numbers when you write. Do not give all the details of this person's life. Discuss only important activities and accomplishments.

Following the Steps in the Writing Process

Before You Write

Step One: *Thinking about the Topic/Getting Ideas*
First, think about the topic choices above. What ideas do you have for each topic? Write as many ideas as you can in the spaces below. Write important dates, numbers, and names. Include notes about accomplishments/achievements for a biography. You do not need to write complete sentences and don't worry about organization for this part.

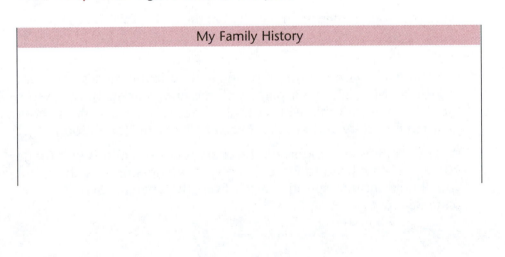

My Family History

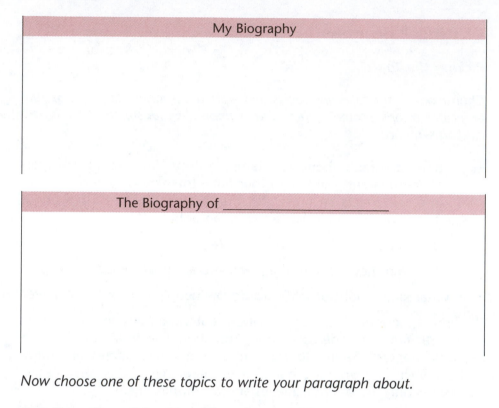

Now choose one of these topics to write your paragraph about.

■   ***Step Two: Organizing Your Thoughts and Ideas***
Think about the main idea of your paragraph.

Topic Sentence

a. What is your topic? Are you going to write about your family history or a biography?

   Topic: _____

b. What is your controlling idea? What part of the topic will you discuss in your supporting sentences?

   Controlling idea: _____

c. Write your topic sentence on the chart at the end of this unit (page 90).

Support

d. Look back at your notes for Step One and circle the details you want to include. Make sure your paragraph has enough details. Make sure the details fit your topic sentence. Also be sure to include facts about your family history and facts and accomplishments for a biography.

e. Write your ideas for support on the chart at the end of this unit (page 90). You do not need to write complete sentences on this chart, but you should include specific words from the chart in Step One on page 85–86.

Concluding Sentence

f. Write a concluding sentence. Remember to restate the main idea of the paragraph or topic sentence. Write this sentence on the chart on page 90.

g. Write a title for this paragraph on the chart at the end of this unit (page 90).

■ *Step Three: Getting Feedback about the Chart*
Show your chart to another person. Your teacher may ask you to work with a partner and complete a review of your chart/outline. Use the review sheet in the Appendix (page 195) for this feedback.

When You Write

■ *Step Four: Writing the First Draft (Rough Draft)*
Write your first draft of the paragraph. Do not worry about perfect grammar, spelling, punctuation, or capitalization for this draft. Make sure you write this first draft using the ideas on the chart/outline (page 90).

Be sure to include the following in your rough draft:
- Write a title.
- Begin the paragraph with a topic sentence.
- Support your topic sentence with facts as well as accomplishments or achievements (for a biography).
- Make sure you have enough support (at least five to seven sentences).
- Use at least three of the coordinating conjunctions you learned in this unit (*and, but, so, or*) in your paragraph.
- Use at least three vocabulary words from this unit.
- End your paragraph with a concluding sentence. (Restate the main idea in this sentence.)

After You Write

Check Your Work
After you finish writing the first draft, read your paragraph again. Check your work for the following. Do this before you show it to anyone else.

☐ This paragraph discusses one of the following:
- my family history
- my biography
- the biography of someone in my family

☐ This paragraph has a title.

☐ This paragraph has a topic sentence.

☐ This paragraph has at least five to seven sentences of support/ details.

☐ All of the details/support relate to the topic sentence.

☐ The support/details include facts, such as names, dates, and numbers.

☐ For a biography I included accomplishments and achievements of this person.

This paragraph has a concluding sentence.

☐ The concluding sentence restates the topic sentence.

☐ I used three vocabulary words from this lesson in the paragraph.

☐ I wrote some simple sentences and some sentences with coordinating conjunctions.

☐ I used three different coordinating conjunctions in my sentences.

☐ I checked my sentences for fragments (missing subjects or verbs).

☐ I checked my sentences for run-ons and comma splices.

This paragraph has correct paragraph form as follows:

☐ The title is centered above the paragraph.

☐ The title has correct capitalization.

☐ The title does not end in a period.

☐ I indented the first sentence of the paragraph.

☐ I have correct margins on the left and right.

☐ I did not put punctuation (period, comma, question mark) at the beginning of a new line.

☐ I double-spaced (skipped a space after every line).

☐ All of my sentences follow one another. (I did not go to the next line with a new sentence.)

■ *Step Five: Getting Feedback about the First Draft*
Show someone your first draft of the paragraph. Your teacher will decide the type of feedback you will receive for the first draft. It may be with a partner or from the teacher or both ways. For review with a partner, use the sheet on pages 196–197 in the Appendix.

■ *Step Six: Making Changes*
After you receive feedback, make some changes. First, decide if you want to change your topic sentence. Then decide if you want to change your supporting sentences by adding new ones or taking out some. Decide if you want to change your concluding sentence.

After you make these changes, look at all the grammar, punctuation, spelling, and capitalization. Make any necessary changes in these things as well.

■ *Step Seven: The Final Draft*
Type your final draft on a computer. Try to make this paragraph as perfect as you can.

Organizing Your Thoughts for Writing

TITLE: _____

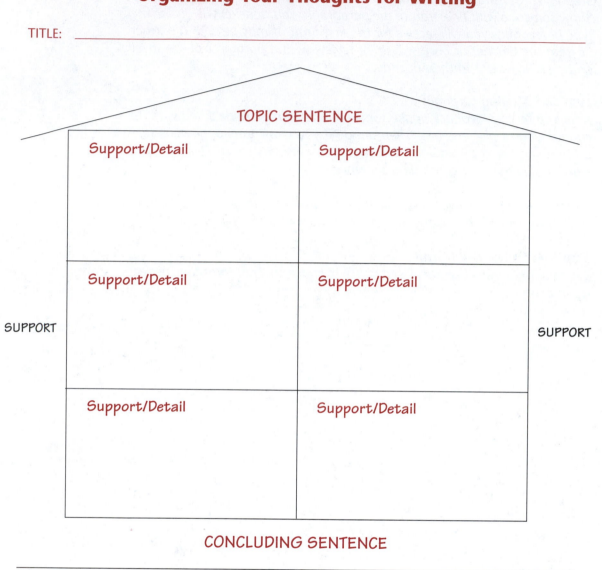

TOPIC SENTENCE

Support/Detail

Support/Detail

SUPPORT

Support/Detail

Support/Detail

SUPPORT

Support/Detail

Support/Detail

CONCLUDING SENTENCE

_____

_____

_____

Jobs and the Workplace

Content Area: Business and Workplace English

Reading: The Changing Workplace

Short Readings: Job Applications
Job Interviews
Replacing a Printer Ink Cartridge

Sentence Writing Focus: Making Connections with Introductory Transitions

Editing Focus: Fragments/Run-ons/Comma Splices

Writing Focus: Paragraphs (Instructions/Procedures/Chronology)
Concluding Sentences

PART 1   UNIT PREVIEW

Preview Activity: Discussion and Office Equipment Identification

A. Answer the following discussion questions.

1. What is a typical work schedule for workers in your native culture or the place where you are now living? How many days of the week and hours each day do people usually work in these places?

2. Do you work or are you a full-time student? What kind of job(s) did you have in the past or do you have now? What was/is your work schedule?

3. What are your work or career goals? How will studying English help you with your job or career?

B. Look at the following photographs of typical office equipment. On the line below each one, write the name of this machine. Do you know how to use all of these?

_____   _____   _____

Share your answers with a partner and/or the class.

Quickwrite/Freewrite

Write for five minutes about the following topic. Do not worry about grammar, spelling, or punctuation. Just write what comes to your mind about the topic.

- *If you could choose one perfect job or career, what would it be? Explain your answer.*

PART 2   READING AND VOCABULARY

Read about how some kinds of jobs are changing and then answer the questions following the reading.

1   Today's workplace is changing quickly because of technological **advances** and increasing **globalization**. These changes are making work at many jobs both challenging and exciting. The challenges may come with the need for learning and understanding new technology in order to stay **competitive** and **productive**. On the other hand, many people are finding exciting new directions for their **careers** because they can take advantage of different **options** in the workplace.

Flexible Workweek

2   The traditional workweek in the United States includes five days of work from 8 or 9 A.M. to 5 P.M. However, this is changing in some companies. Some businesses are establishing more flexible work hours to **accommodate** changing family situations and employee needs.

3   Some companies offer a **compressed workweek**. This means employees work the usual number of hours per week (usually 35 to 40 hours), but they work fewer days. Thus, a 40-hour week may **consist of** 4 days of ten hours of work each day.

4   Flextime is another change from traditional work hours. In this case work hours are **staggered,** so all employees do not arrive or leave work at the same time. For example, some employees may come to work at 7:30 A.M. and leave at 4 P.M., and others may arrive at 8 or 8:30 A.M. and leave at 4:30 or 5 P.M. In this way certain hours are **core hours,** or times that everyone is in the office, but employees have some flexibility in their schedules.

5   A third nontraditional work schedule is job sharing. Under this arrangement two part-time employees accomplish the work of a job that one full-time employee usually holds. In this situation two people might each work five half days or one person could work three full days, and the other would work the other two days.

Virtual Office

6   Through technology some office **professionals** may be physically in one place and **virtually** in another. In other words, workers can communicate through technology, such as the Internet or **interactive** television with people in places far away. This kind of work may involve going to the company office for part of the time, working at home some of the time, or even working **exclusively** at home. In addition, someone may work this way for a specific company, or s/he may be self-employed.

Telecommuting

7   Telecommuting is very similar to the virtual office. However, in telecommuting the individual always works for a specific organization or employer. This kind of job involves individuals

working at home, at a customer's office, or at some location outside the main office of the business. Communicating with the main office occurs through computers or other technological equipment, such as fax machines or cellular phones.

Contracted Specialists

8　Not all employees in large companies are full-time, regular employees. Some individuals are **freelance** specialists, and they move from organization to organization to perform jobs with agreements or on contract. These individuals may be working mainly in their home offices or virtual offices, so they visit the contractor's office only occasionally.

Comprehension Check

Main Ides

Circle the letter of your answer for each of the following.

1. The main idea of this reading is:

    a. In today's workplace most employees have nontraditional schedules and jobs using new technology.

    b. All companies are changing many things, such as technological equipment and new kinds of jobs for employees.

    c. In today's workplace you might find several new kinds of schedules and jobs for some workers.

2. This reading discusses how workers can

    a. change the hours they start and end a workday.

    b. have nontraditional work schedules and ways to do their jobs.

    c. work with computers and cell phones.

Details

A. Label the following as True (T) or False (F) according to the reading.

_____ 1. Today's changes in the workplace are the result of people's use of computers only.

_____ 2. Workers today need to continue to educate themselves about new machines and equipment.

_____ 3. In the United States most people usually work five days a week for about eight to nine hours a day.

_____ 4. Today any employee of any company can ask for a nontraditional work schedule, and s/he will surely get it.

B. Match the characteristics with the schedule or job type they describe according to the reading. Write the letter of the characteristic on the line given and use each characteristic at least once. In some cases you may choose more than one characteristic. Follow the example.

Schedules

1. compressed workweek   _____
2. flextime   _____
3. job sharing   _a_____

Characteristics

a. More than one worker completes the work for one job.

b. Some employees come to work earlier than others.

c. Employees work a full 40-hour week but in fewer than five days.

d. Some employees leave work later than others.

e. Employees work only part of the week and not the full 40 hours.

Job Types

1. virtual office   _____
2. telecommuting   _____
3. contracted specialists   _____

Characteristics

a. The employee may work for several companies or organizations.

b. The employee may work at home only.

c. The employee may work at home sometimes and in the office sometimes.

d. Two people may work together, but they are not both in the same place.

e. The employee works for himself and is not a regular employee of the company.

f. The employee works for one specific company.

Vocabulary Study

A. Below you will find an underlined vocabulary word from the reading in each sentence and four definitions or synonyms after that sentence. Circle the two choices that have the same meaning as the vocabulary word. Follow the example.

1. International companies and the use of technology are creating more and more <u>globalization</u> for many companies.

    a. use of maps

    (b.) working worldwide

    c. local

    (d.) developing an economy through worldwide business

2. Sometimes very <u>productive</u> workers will get extra money or another type of reward.

    a. able to create or make something

    b. intelligent

    c. able to use technology easily

    d. able to get results

3. Some people go back to school in order to find a new kind of work and <u>career.</u>

    a. temporary job

    b. education

    c. job one trains for as a profession

    d. life's work

4. Mary was very happy about all the work <u>options</u> available to her after she received her college degree.

    a. choices

    b. jobs

    c. alternatives

    d. schedules

5. Some employees like to have <u>flexible</u> work schedules so that they can easily take care of things outside of work when necessary.

    a. unable to change

    b. able to change

    c. not rigid or always the same

    d. always the same

6. Many places have laws to <u>accommodate</u> disabled people both in buildings and public places.

    a. make fit or suitable

    b. help out

    c. leave out

    d. give money to

B. Choose a definition/synonym from the following list for each of the underlined vocabulary words in the sentences. Write the letter of the answer on the line next to the sentence. The first one has been done as an example.

a. improvements/progress

b. ~~only/limited to one thing~~

c. are made up of/include

d. occurring between different people or groups; two-way communication

e. independent worker/not working for one employer

f. able to work against others to get something

g. someone working on a job with specialized knowledge and standards __b__ 1. On Bill's new job he works <u>exclusively</u> with international companies.

____ 2. Ingrid is majoring in business in school because she wants to be an office <u>professional</u>.

____ 3. Businesses must be <u>competitive</u> if they want to have many customers and make money.

____ 4. Most big businesses <u>consist of</u> different kinds of employees, such as managers, supervisors, sales people, and secretaries.

____ 5. Some instructors prefer to have <u>interactive</u> lessons in their classes, so they don't like to be the only person talking for the whole class time.

____ 6. We make <u>advances</u> in machines and communication, and these help business in many ways.

____ 7. Janet loves her job as a <u>freelance</u> computer technician because it gives her many interesting experiences with different companies.

C. *Match the words/expressions in Column A with their meanings in Column B. If you are not sure of these meanings, look back at the paragraph number given in parentheses in Column A. Then read the paragraph again for an explanation.*

A	B
____ 1. compressed workweek (3)	a. workers for one company communicate with each other or the central office through technology
____ 2. staggered work hours (4)	b. central or basic work times when all workers are present
____ 3. core hours (4)	c. works independently by agreement, not as a regular employee of the company
____ 4. virtually (6)	d. reduced/condensed time for work
____ 5. telecommuting (7)	e. not in reality or physically, but through technology
____ 6. contracted specialist (8)	f. variety of start and end times for work

Discussion/Writing

Your teacher will tell you to answer these questions in writing or through discussion.

1. When you work a full-time job, would you like to have one of the flexible work schedules described in the reading? Which one do you prefer and why?

2. What do you think about each of the following: working in a virtual office, telecommuting, working as a contract/freelance specialist? Do you see any problems with these kinds of jobs? Explain your answer.

PART 3   WRITING SENTENCES—MAKING CONNECTIONS WITH TRANSITIONS

Read the paragraph about job applications and answer the questions that follow.

Reading

Job Applications

[1]An application provides an employer with several kinds of information about an applicant, so it is important to fill out this form carefully. [2]Employers read these forms to help choose the right person for a position in their workplace. [3]For one thing, often employers will "screen out" applicants for interviews by reading their applications. [4]In other words, they will choose people to interview from the information on these forms. [5]In addition, sometimes there may be as many as 100 applications for one job opening. [6]As a result, the employer may go through these papers quickly in order to find the applicants' strong points and abilities. [7]The application must give the employer a good enough impression for him/her to want to speak to the applicant personally at an interview. [8]Employers usually do not want to see blank spaces on these forms, so applicants should fill out everything completely. [9]On the other hand, they should be careful about writing too much or giving unrelated or untruthful information just to fill in spaces. [10]Furthermore, an employer may think of an application as an example of the quality of the applicant's work. [11]Therefore, the appearance of the form should always be neat and clean, and the information should be easy to read. [12]Filling out an application carefully and accurately will give an employer important information to help make decisions about an applicant.

Questions

1. Circle the expression at the beginning of sentence 3. You learned in Unit One that this is a transition. What does it mean? How is it related to the information in sentence 2?

2. Sentences 5 and 10 also begin with transitions. Circle these words or expressions. These two transitions have the same meaning. What is this meaning?

3. Sentences 6 and 11 also begin with transitions. Circle these words or expressions. These two transitions have the same meaning. What is this meaning?

Explanation—Using Introductory Transitions

1. In Unit Three you learned to combine sentences (clauses) using coordinating conjunctions to show a relationship between the two ideas.

    EXAMPLE: An application provides an employer with several kinds of information about an applicant, **so** it is important to fill out this form carefully.   result

    The appearance of the form should always be neat and clean, **and** the information should be easy to read.

    more information

2. Transitions also show a relationship between sentences. They make a connection or bridge between ideas (*trans* = across). Not every sentence needs a transition, but a good writer uses some transitions to make sentences flow more smoothly. Without transitions, sentences may seem choppy or to jump from one idea to another without a clear relationship.

    There are several different ways a writer can use transitions. In this book you will learn about transitions at the beginning of a sentence, or *introductory transitions*. When we use introductory transitions, we also write a comma after them.

3. Transitions have specific meanings. In Unit One you learned about several transitions as follows:

    a. Introductory transitions showing examples

        for example   for instance   for one thing

    EXAMPLES: **For one thing,** often an employer will "screen out" applicants for interviews by reading their applications.

    Employers use applications to make decisions about applicants. **For example/For instance,** they may choose applicants to interview from the information on their papers.

    b. Introductory transitions showing more information

        in addition   also   furthermore

    EXAMPLES: **In addition,** sometimes there may be as many as 100 applications for one job opening.

    Furthermore, an employer may think of an application as an example of the quality of the applicant's work.

4. There are many other transitions.

a. Transitions showing contrast or opposite

however   *on the other hand*

EXAMPLE: Applicants should fill out their papers completely. **However/ On the other hand,** they should not fill in spaces with unre- lated or untruthful information.

b. Transition showing result

therefore   *thus*   *as a result*

EXAMPLE: An employer may think of an application as an example of the quality of the applicant's work. **Therefore/Thus/As a result,** the appearance of the form should always be neat and clean.

c. Transition showing a restatement/review of something with the same meaning (using different words)

in other words

EXAMPLE: Often employers will "screen out" applicants for interviews by reading their applications. **In other words,** they will choose people to interview from the information on these forms.

5. **Important—Errors to Avoid**

Editing Focus

Fragments, Run-ons, Comma Splices

a. **Fragments**

- Be sure to have a complete sentence (clause) with a subject and verb after an introductory transition.

INCORRECT: The applicant must give the employer a good impression. Therefore, a neat and complete application. fragment (no verb)

CORRECT: The applicant must give the employer a good impression. Therefore, a neat and complete application is important.

- *Such as* is not an introductory transition and should not begin a sentence. Using *such as* at the beginning of a sentence will make a fragment.

INCORRECT: There are many things an employer thinks about before hiring someone. **Such as** the applicant's education and work experience.

CORRECT: There are many things an employer thinks about before hiring someone, **such as** the applicant's education and work experience.

Note the use of a comma just before the *such as* in the correct example.

b. **Run-ons**   Do not use an introductory transition between clauses. These transitions should come at the beginning of a sentence.*

INCORRECT: An employer may think of an application as an example of the quality of the applicant's work therefore the

run on

appearance of the form should always be neat and clean.

CORRECT: An employer may think of an application as an example of the quality of the applicant's work. Therefore, the appearance of the form should always be neat and clean.

c. **Comma splices**   Do not use an introductory transition between clauses with a comma. These transitions should come at the beginning of a sentence.

INCORRECT: An employer may think of an application as an example of the quality of the applicant's work, therefore the

comma splice

appearance of the form should always be neat and clean.

CORRECT: An employer may think of an application as an example of the quality of the applicant's work. Therefore, the appearance of the form should always be neat and clean.

Practice: Using Introductory Transitions

A. Identifying Introductory Transitions   *Circle the transition in each sentence. Then indicate the kind of relationship this transition is showing by choosing the correct letter from the choices listed below. Follow the example.*

a. example
b. to review
c. more information
d. opposite
e. result

___c___ 1. An applicant should fill out an application completely. In addition, s/he must be honest and accurate with all the answers.

_____ 2. An employer wants to see if the applicant can follow instructions. Therefore, filling out the application correctly is very important.

_____ 3. It is important to read all instructions before writing anything on an application. In other words, the applicant should not answer the questions before reading through the form.

_____ 4. A neat and complete application suggests a good worker to an employer. On the other hand, a messy or incomplete form gives a bad impression.

---

*Note: Linking transitions combine sentences/clauses. In this book you will practice using introductory transitions only. Destinations, Level 2, will discuss and practice linking transitions.

_____ 5. Some employers may consider some parts of an application more important than others. For instance, they may be very interested in the past jobs of an applicant.

B. *Matching Sentences with Logical Relationships*   *Match the sentence in column A with the sentence that best follows it in B. Use each answer only one time.*

<table>
<tr><td align="center">A</td><td align="center">B</td></tr>
<tr><td>_____ 1. An applicant should fill out the application completely.</td><td>a. Thus, s/he should not write anything negative in the answers.</td></tr>
<tr><td>_____ 2. The applicant wants to make a good impression on the application.</td><td>b. Furthermore, they may ask reasons for leaving those jobs.</td></tr>
<tr><td>_____ 3. An applicant may be willing to take any job available.</td><td>c. In other words, s/he should not leave any blank spaces.</td></tr>
<tr><td>_____ 4. Sometimes an applicant can say a question is not related to him/her.</td><td>d. However, it is not a good idea to say "open" or "anything available" on the form.</td></tr>
<tr><td>_____ 5. Most job applications ask for information about previous jobs.</td><td>e. For example, s/he can write, "does not apply" or "not applicable."</td></tr>
</table>

C. *Choosing the Transition—Meanings*

1. Circle the transition in parentheses that makes the best relationship between the two sentences after each number. Then write the second sentence on the line given using the transition you chose. Be sure to use correct punctuation and capitalization. Follow the example.

   a. An application may be messy in several ways.

   An applicant may change answers by using white out or black lines. (for example/on the other hand)

   For example, an applicant may change answers using white out or black lines.

   b. Applicants should write neatly or type all answers.

   They should not erase or cross anything out. (in sum/also)

   _____

   c. An employer may receive many applications for one job.

   Some of them might be difficult to read or understand. (in other words/however)

   _____

d. Crossing out and making many erasures make an application look messy.

An employer might think the applicant is disorganized or not a careful worker. (for example/ as a result)

_____

e. Employers often consider interviewing applicants with neat and complete papers.

Applicants should fill out applications as carefully as possible. (therefore/however)

_____

f. An application usually gives the employer a first idea about the applicant.

It is the applicant's chance to make a good first impression. (for example/in other words)

_____

2. _Rewrite the second sentence next to each number below by starting with a transition that shows the meaning given in parentheses. Be sure to use correct punctuation and capitalization in your answer. Follow the example._

a. Honesty is very important in a job application. Applicants should never lie about anything on their papers. (same meaning)

   In other words, applicants should never lie about anything on their

   papers.

b. An applicant should be prepared to fill out an application in an office. S/he can bring a "fact" sheet with necessary information about past jobs, etc. (example)

_____

c. Applicants should have references available during a job search. They should have those names and contact numbers ready to put on an application. (more information)

_____

d. Having the names and phone numbers of references is important. Applicants should not give out this information before talking to these people. (contrast)

_____

e. A complete and accurate application will make a good impression. Applicants should check their answers before handing in the paper. (result)

_____

D. **Filling in the Correct Transition** *Fill in the spaces in the paragraph that follows with one of the transitions given on the list. Use each transition only once.*

Therefore For example In other words However In addition

It is important to fill out an application completely and honestly. _____, in some cases an applicant may not want to answer a question. _____, sometimes an answer to a question may seem negative and require explanation. _____, someone may have a difficult situation to explain on an application. In these cases an applicant may want to discuss the answer more fully in person. _____, in order to be honest, the applicant can say "will discuss at interview" for a specific question. An applicant should never lie on an application. _____, it is better to write nothing or ask to explain later than to be dishonest on an application.

E. **Completing Sentences on Your Own** *Review the reading in Part 2 (pages 93–94) and complete this exercise with information according to that reading. Using the introductory transition given, write a complete sentence that logically follows the first one. Be sure to use your own words in your answers and include correct punctuation and capitalization. There may be several possible good answers. Follow the example.*

1. The workplace is changing quickly because of many technological advances.

   (in addition) <u>In addition, globalization is causing changes.</u> OR

   <u>In addition, these changes are helping people find new directions in their careers.</u> OR

   <u>In addition, these changes are giving many new options to workers.</u>

2. A compressed workweek requires the usual 35 to 40 hours of work from one employee.

   (however)

3. Some places of work have staggered work hours for employees.

   (as a result)

4. Sometimes two employees work in a job-sharing situation.

   (in other words)

5. Some workers must go to an office every day for work.

   (on the other hand)

6. Telecommuting workers may communicate on their jobs through technology.

   (for example)

7. Virtual office work means the worker does not have to be in one specific place each day.

(for instance)

8. Contracted specialists are not full-time, regular employees at a company.

(therefore)

9. A freelance specialist works on a contract.

(furthermore)

 F. ***Finding Sentence Problems***   *Each of the following paragraphs has one fragment, one comma splice, one run-on, and one mistake with capitalization. Find all the mistakes and correct them.*

1. Some people can start a new job right away, therefore, they write "available immediately" on an application. on the other hand, some applicants already have a job and cannot start immediately. Those people should be polite and respectful to their current employers in other words they should not just leave the job immediately. They should give their current employer notice of their leaving. Such as two weeks before the start of the new job.

2. In the United States employers usually cannot ask for certain kinds of information on an application for one thing, an applicant does not have to give his/her age or date of birth. In a few cases an employer can ask about an applicant's age, for instance, it is okay to ask about a minor or underage person. in addition, most applications do not ask about race, religion, or national origin. Furthermore, there are several laws about hiring people with disabilities. Therefore, must be careful about asking questions about those.

Discussion/Writing

Your teacher will tell you to answer these questions in writing or through discussion.

1. Applications are necessary for many things, including jobs and schools. What applications do you have experience filling out in English? What were the most difficult or confusing parts for you to answer?

2. Imagine you are applying for your ideal job. How might you explain your background, education, and experience for this job? Think about all the positive things you can say about your skills, abilities, and experience.

PART 4   WRITING PARAGRAPHS—(INSTRUCTION PROCEDURES CHRONOLOGY)/ CONCLUDING SENTENCES

Read the following paragraph about a procedure to follow for a job interview and then answer the questions that follow.

Job Interviews

An interview is a chance to sell yourself to an employer, and the following procedure can make the experience a successful one. First, you should get ready for the interview by taking stock of yourself. In other words, you should think about your strongest abilities and qualities. This will help you on the interview and later at the workplace. Second, preparing for the questions and answers is very important. For instance, you can research both the company and the job. Also, you could practice answering possible interview questions. This might include preparing a short review of your strengths, background, and goals. Next, it is important to make a good impression during the interview, so you should make sure you present yourself well in person. For one thing, you should dress appropriately for the type of business and job. In addition, you should arrive a little early for your appointment. During the interview it is important to present your information and interest in the job with a positive attitude. Finally, after the interview it is a good idea to send a thank-you note. This will help the interviewer remember you and can make you "different" from the other candidates for the job. In sum, following this procedure of preparation, good interview practices, and follow-up can help you get the job.

Paragraph Discussion

1. Does this paragraph follow correct paragraph format? Does it have all of the following?

    ___ a title centered above the paragraph

    ___ correct capitalization of the title

    ___ indenting of the first sentence

    ___ each sentence following the one before

    ___ correct left and right margins

    ___ a capital letter at the beginning of each new sentence

    ___ end punctuation for each sentence

2. Does this paragraph have a topic sentence? What is the main idea of this paragraph?

3. What kind of information do the supporting sentences give?

4. Circle all the introductory transitions from Part 3 of this unit in this paragraph.

5. Does this paragraph have a concluding sentence? What kind of information does the last sentence give?

Paragraph Organization—Using Chronology with Instructions/Procedures

Writing Focus

Paragraph Organization: Chronology with Instructions/ Procedures

1. We often find instructions and procedures in many situations in our daily life, including the workplace, school, and home, etc. Instructions and procedures explain how things are done and are often necessary to be successful in daily activities or duties.

2. Instructions and procedures usually follow specific steps. These steps may require a certain order because one step must come before another. We call this *chronological* order or *chronology,* and we often use introductory transitions to show this kind of order.

3. There are several common introductory transitions that show chronological order, as follows.

   first (first of all)   second   then   next   later   finally

   First, you should get ready for the interview by taking stock of yourself.

   Second, preparing for the questions and answers is very important.

   Next, it is important to make a good impression during the interview, so you should make sure you present yourself well in person.

   Finally, after the interview it is a good idea to send a thank-you note.

Use these introductory transitions the same way you learned to use the transitions in Part 3 of this unit. In other words, put these words and expressions at the beginning of a sentence and follow them with a comma. Sometimes you will see the introductory transition *then* without a comma, but you should use commas with the others.

Practice: Chronology with Instructions/Procedures

1. Look at the following information about two different procedures. For each procedure label the topic sentence with the letters TS and then give each supporting sentence a number to show correct order. Begin with number 1 for the first step and end with number 5 for the last step.

PROCEDURE: RETRIEVING VOICE MAIL MESSAGES

___ a. You will hear some instructions to give your extension number and password.

___ b. In this company, getting your voice mail messages from an outside phone is not a difficult procedure.

___ c. To end the call, you need to press the star button.

___ d. You must dial the number for voice mail access (555–1128).

___ e. Follow the instructions for saving, deleting, or responding to each message.

___ f. You push the number seven to hear any new messages.

2. *Now do the same for the following information about packaging things for shipment.*

PROCEDURE: PACKAGING PRODUCTS FOR SHIPMENT

___ a. You will apply one preprinted shipping label to each sealed carton.

___ b. You need to cover the contents of each filled box with packing material.

___ c. You must fill each carton with one dozen bags of product.

___ d. Packing products for shipment from this company requires a specific procedure.

___ e. You have to place each packed carton on a shipping pallet for movement into the warehouse.

___ f. In order to seal each carton, close the top flaps and place sealing tape across the top.

Paragraph Organization—Support for Procedures/Instructions and Concluding Sentences

1. Support: As you learned in the first three units, it is important to have enough details to support the topic sentence of your paragraph. In Unit One you learned about supporting examples by writing more than one sentence to explain each example. It is a good idea to write more than one sentence to explain each step in a procedure or instruction as well. This will help the reader more fully understand and be able to perform the task.

2. Concluding Sentences: As you learned in Unit Three, often the last sentence in the paragraph is a concluding sentence. Sometimes this

sentence will be a restatement of the topic sentence/main idea. Other times the concluding sentence will give a short review or summary of the information in the paragraph. This kind of concluding sentence should be a general review. In the case of instructions or a procedure, it could be a general review of the steps. Do not include just one detail or one step from the paragraph in a concluding sentence.

Look back at the concluding sentence of the model paragraph about job interviews (page 106) and underline it. How does this sentence give a general review of the steps in the paragraph?

3. There are some introductory transitions you can use when you write this kind of concluding sentence, as follows.

in short   in brief   in summary   in sum

Use these introductory transitions the same way you learned to use the other transitions of this unit.

In sum, following this procedure of preparation, good interview practices, and follow up can help you get the job.

Practice: Paragraph Organization—Topic Sentences, Chronological Support, and Concluding Sentences

A. Identifying Support for Steps in a Procedure

1. Look back at the paragraph about job interviews (page 106) and do the following:

a. Put a box around all the introductory transitions that show chronological order. How many specific steps are in this procedure?

b. Put a line under each sentence that gives extra information about one of the steps. Follow the example for the first one below.

First, you should get ready for the interview by taking stock of yourself. <u>In other words, you should think about your strongest abilities and qualities. This will help you on the interview and later at the workplace.</u>

B. Identifying Parts of a Paragraph and Choosing a Conclusion
Read the following paragraph about replacing a used ink cartridge in a printer. Then complete the exercise that follows.

Replacing a Printer Ink Cartridge

Replacing a used ink cartridge in a printer with a new one takes only a few minutes by following a short procedure. First, you should press the "on" button of the printer. Many printers will not move the cartridge to the correct position without this first step. Second, you must open the access door of the printer and find the cartridge. You should see it easily either in the middle or to one side. Next, you may need to lift a cover from the cartridge before removing it. For some printers, there is no cover, so you can simply take the cartridge out of the machine. Then you need to pull the pink tab on the new cartridge to remove the piece of tape covering part of it. You should make sure not to touch the copper-colored contacts and never retape the cartridge. Next, you should insert the new cartridge in the empty slot with the label on top. You will hear it snap into place. Finally, close the access door and look for any other instructions on the printer. For example, it may direct you to press a button for print alignment or a test page.

1. Look back at the paragraph and do the following:

   a. Put a line under the topic sentence.

   b. Circle the introductory transitions that show chronological order. How many steps does this paragraph discuss?

   c. Put a line under every sentence that gives extra information about one of the steps.

2. Circle the letter of the concluding sentence that best gives a review or summary of steps in the paragraph. Be prepared to explain your answer.

   a. In short, following this procedure of carefully removing the old cartridge and properly inserting the new one will make the task an easy one.

   b. In brief, replacing a used ink cartridge in a printer with a new one is fast and easy by following this short procedure.

   c. In summary, taking off the tape and putting the new cartridge in the correct slot can be very important parts of this procedure.

C. Writing a Complete Paragraph

1. Look back at the practice with chronology about voice mail messages and packaging products for shipment (page 108). Choose one of those two procedures/instructions and write the information in a paragraph with all the parts on the lines provided on the next page.

Use the following instructions to write your paragraph:

a. Write the title.

b. Begin the paragraph with the topic sentence given.

c. Write each step in the correct order after the topic sentence. Begin these steps with as many of the following introductory transitions as possible. Use the following:

first (first of all)   second   then   next   later   finally

d. What kind of information can you add about some of these steps? Add one more sentence to at least two of the steps in this paragraph to explain them in more detail. You may use some of the introductory transitions from Part 3 of this unit (pages 98–101) for these sentences as well.

e. End the paragraph with a concluding sentence. This sentence should provide a review or summary of the steps in the procedure/ instructions.

Title: _____

_____

_____

_____

_____

_____

_____

_____

_____

_____

_____

_____

2. The following steps are in correct order for filling out a job application. Read them and then follow the instructions for writing this information as a good paragraph.

- Before you begin, you should be sure you have a good pen to write your answers.

- You should also bring a fact sheet of dates and names of employers and references with you.

- It is always a good idea to read *all* the instructions before writing anything on the application.

- You need to complete all the spaces completely and accurately.

- You must read all the information on the paper before signing at the end.

- You should always check your paper carefully before handing it in.

- You can give your paper to the employer if you are sure it is as complete and accurate as possible.

Use the sentences above to write a good paragraph as follows: (Use the lines provided below).

a. Write a title for this paragraph.

b. Begin the paragraph with a topic sentence.

c. Write each step in order after the topic sentence. Begin at least three of your sentences with one of the following transitions. Use at least three different transitions.

   first (first of all)   second   then   next   later   finally

d. Add at least one more sentence to some of the steps in this paragraph to explain those steps in more detail. You may use some of the introductory transitions from Part 3 of this unit (pages 98–101) for these sentences as well.

e. End the paragraph with a concluding sentence. This sentence should provide a review or summary of the steps in the procedure.

Title: _____

_____

_____

_____

_____

_____

_____

_____

_____

_____

_____

_____

_____

Discussion/Writing

Your teacher will tell you to answer these questions in writing or through discussion.

1. What experience(s) did you have in the past with job interviews or an interview for something else, such as something for school? How did you prepare for this interview? Discuss your experience using chronological order.

2. What is the best way for you to follow directions in English: through listening to them or through reading them? Explain your answer.

Writing Assignment

Picking the Topic

Choose one of the following topics and write a paragraph. Be sure to include a topic sentence, steps in chronological order (using transitions), and a concluding sentence that reviews or summarizes the steps in the paragraph.

1. Write a paragraph giving instructions to operate or use a machine or piece of equipment that you know well.

2. Write a paragraph discussing a procedure you know well. It can be something you do at home, at school, or at work.

NOTE: Try to choose a simple set of instructions or procedure. In other words, limit your instructions/procedure to no more than six or seven steps.

Following the Steps in the Writing Process

Before You Write

Step One: Thinking about the Topic/Getting Ideas
First, think about the writing assignments. What ideas do you have for each topic? Choose a machine, a piece of equipment, or a procedure that you know well and write that on the space given for each topic. Then write as many ideas as you can in the space below the topic. Write the steps and be sure to keep them in chronological order. Include information that explains as many steps as possible. You do not need to write complete sentences and don't worry about organization for this part.

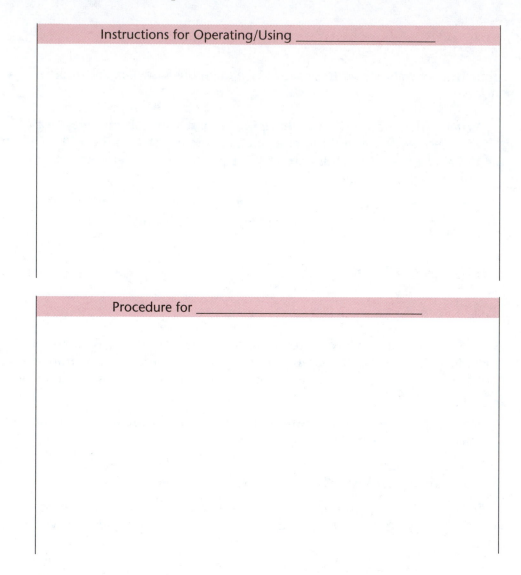

Instructions for Operating/Using _____

Procedure for _____

Now choose one of these topics to write your paragraph about.

■ *Step Two: Organizing Your Thoughts and Ideas*
Think about the main idea of your paragraph.

Topic Sentence

a. What is your topic? Are you going to write about operating/using a machine or piece of equipment or about a familiar procedure?

Topic: _____

b. What is your controlling idea? What will you discuss in your supporting sentences for these instructions or this procedure?

Controlling idea: _____

c. Write your topic sentence on the chart at the end of this unit (page 118).

Support

d. Look back at your notes for Step One and circle the steps/details you want to include. Make sure your paragraph has enough support. Make sure the steps fit your topic sentence and be sure to include them in chronological order. Also, be sure to have some details that explain the steps.

e. Write your ideas for support on the chart at the end of this unit (page 118). You do not need to write complete sentences on this chart, but you should include specific words from your notes in Step One on page 114.

Concluding Sentence

f. Write a concluding sentence. Be sure to review or summarize the steps of the paragraph in this sentence. Write this sentence on the chart on page 118.

g. Write a title for this paragraph on the chart at the end of this unit (page 118).

■ **Step Three: Getting Feedback about the Chart**
Show your chart to another person. Your teacher may ask you to work with a partner and complete a review of your chart/outline. Use the review sheet in the Appendix (page 198) for this feedback.

<u>When You Write</u>

■ **Step Four: Writing the First Draft (Rough Draft)**
Write your first draft of the paragraph. Do not worry about perfect grammar, spelling, punctuation, or capitalization for this draft. Make sure you write this first draft using the ideas on the chart/outline (page 118).

Be sure to include the following in your rough draft:
• Write a title.
• Begin the paragraph with a topic sentence.
• Support your topic sentence with the steps in the instructions or procedure.
• Make sure you have enough support to fully explain the instructions or procedure. This support should be in chronological order.
• Use at least three introductory transitions to show chronological order in your paragraph.
• Use at least three of the other introductory transitions you learned in Part 3 of this unit in your paragraph.
• Use at least three of the coordinating conjunctions you learned in Unit Three (*and, but, so, or*).
• Try to use at least three vocabulary words from this unit.
• End your paragraph with a concluding sentence that reviews or summarizes the paragraph.

After You Write

Check Your Work

After you finish writing the first draft, read your paragraph again. Check your work for the following. Do this before you show it to anyone else.

☐ This paragraph discusses one of the following:

- instructions for using a machine or piece of equipment
- a procedure I am familiar with

☐ This paragraph has a title.

☐ This paragraph has a topic sentence.

☐ This paragraph has at least four or five steps for the instructions/ procedure.

☐ All of the steps relate to the topic sentence.

☐ The steps are in chronological order.

☐ I explained some of the steps with more supporting sentences.

☐ This paragraph has a concluding sentence.

☐ The concluding sentence reviews/summarizes the steps.

☐ I used three vocabulary words from this lesson in the paragraph.

☐ I used at least three introductory transitions showing chronological order in this paragraph.

☐ I used at least three other introductory transitions in this paragraph.

☐ I wrote some simple sentences and some sentences with coordinating conjunctions.

☐ I used three different coordinating conjunctions in my sentences.

☐ I used several different introductory transitions, including some of chronological order.

☐ I checked my sentences for fragments (missing subjects or verbs).

☐ I checked my sentences for run-ons and comma splices.

This paragraph has the correct paragraph form as follows:

☐ The title is centered above the paragraph.

☐ The title has correct capitalization.

☐ The title does not end in a period.

☐ I indented the first sentence of the paragraph.

☐ I have correct margins on the left and right.

☐ I did not put punctuation (period, comma, question mark) at the beginning of a new line.

☐ I double-spaced (skipped a space after every line).

☐ All of my sentences follow one another. (I did not go to the next line with a new sentence.)

■ *Step Five: Getting Feedback about the First Draft*
Show someone your first draft of the paragraph. Your teacher will decide the type of feedback you will receive for the first draft. It may be with a partner or from the teacher or both ways. For review with a partner, use the sheet on pages 199–200 in the Appendix.

■ *Step Six: Making Changes*
After you receive feedback, make some changes. First, decide if you want to change your topic sentence. Then decide if you want to change your supporting sentences by adding new ones or taking out some. Decide if you want to change your concluding sentence.

After you make these changes, look at all the grammar, punctuation, spelling, and capitalization. Make any necessary changes in these things as well.

■ *Step Seven: The Final Draft*
Type your final draft on a computer. Try to make this paragraph as perfect as you can.

Organizing Your Thoughts for Writing

TITLE: _____

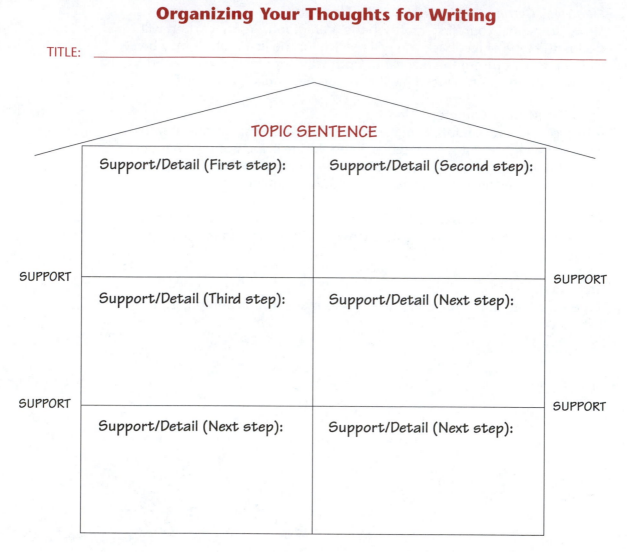

TOPIC SENTENCE

Support/Detail (First step):	Support/Detail (Second step):
Support/Detail (Third step):	Support/Detail (Next step):
Support/Detail (Next step):	Support/Detail (Next step):

SUPPORT · SUPPORT · SUPPORT · SUPPORT

CONCLUDING SENTENCE

_____
_____
_____

Technology and Education

Content Area: Science and Technology

Reading: Distance Education/Learning

Short Readings: Technology in the Classroom
Tips for Taking Online Classes
Distance Learning: An Excellent Educational
Experience
No Laptops in the Classroom

Sentence Writing Focus: Combining Sentences with Subordinating
Conjunctions (*because / if*)

Editing Focus: Run-ons/Comma Splices/Fragments

Writing Focus: Paragraphs (Opinions and Reasons)
Supporting Sentences

PART 1 UNIT PREVIEW

Preview Activity: Questionnaire: Is Distance Education Right for You?

Complete all three parts of this questionnaire. Then read the explanations that follow to see if distance education might be good for you.

A. Basic Requirements
Write True (T) or False (F) for the following statements.

_____ 1. I have a computer, or I can get to one very easily.

_____ 2. I can get to the Internet on the computer I use.

_____ 3. Typing is not a big problem for me.

_____ 4. Reading in English is not a problem for me.

B. Ability to Use a Computer
Answer yes or no to the following questions about your ability to use computers and the Internet.

_____ 1. In general, I am comfortable using a computer and the Internet.

_____ 2. I can use Internet email and the World Wide Web (www) seven days a week.

_____ 3. I know how to send and receive email messages.

_____ 4. I can attach a file to an email message.

_____ 5. I am able to use standard computer programs, such as word processing and spreadsheets.

_____ 6. I can create, save, and manage my own files on a computer.

C. Personal Learning Needs and Preferences
Circle the letter of the answer that best fits you and your needs/preferences.

1. Which of the following describes your work habits?

   a. I usually complete my work/assignments on time or before the due date.

   b. People need to remind me to complete my work.

   c. I often wait until the last minute to complete work, and sometimes I am late with it.

2. When I get a new assignment at work or at school, I prefer to

   a. figure out the instructions completely by myself.

   b. try to follow the directions and then ask for help if I need it.

   c. have the instructor or supervisor explain everything to me.

3. If I need help understanding a subject I am studying,

   a. I feel comfortable going to an instructor to ask for some help.

   b. I feel uncomfortable going to an instructor, but I do it anyway.

   c. I never go to an instructor to ask for help.

4. Coming to campus on a regular schedule is

   a. very difficult for me because of family and/or work.

   b. a little difficult, but I can manage it.

   c. easy for me.

5. Feeling part of a class is

   a. not important at all to me.

   b. a little important to me.

   c. very important to me.

Answers and scoring

A. You should answer *True* for all four of these questions. If you answered *False* for any of them, distance education might be difficult for you at this time.

B. You should be able to answer *yes* for at least four of these questions. If you answered *no* for more than two of these, you might not be ready for distance education.

C. Scoring: A = 3 points   B = 2 points   C = 1 point

   If you scored a total of 10 points or more, you could be a good distance learner. If you scored between 5 and 10 points, distance learning might be good for you, but you may have to make a few changes in your schedule or study habits. If you scored 4 points or less, distance learning may not be a good choice for you at this time.

Quickwrite/Freewrite

Write for five minutes about the following topic. Do not worry about grammar, spelling, or punctuation. Just write what comes to your mind about the topic.

- How comfortable are you using computers and the Internet? Do you find computers easy to use for school? What do you think about using the Internet for your studies?

PART 2   READING AND VOCABULARY

Reading

Distance
Education/Learning

Our technological abilities today go far beyond the abilities of previous generations. Machines and **devices**, such as computers, cell phones, PDAs (personal digital assistants), GPSs (global positioning systems), and many other modern **conveniences** play a part in the everyday lives of millions of people around the world. People use computers for work, school, and **recreation** in many ways. In fact, many schools are now offering courses to students through the use of computers and **access** to the Internet and World Wide Web (www). These courses, called distance education or distance learning, are bringing education to many people who may not be able to take classes in any other way.

What is Distance Education/Distance Learning?

Many schools offer students the flexibility of taking courses without coming to campus on a regular basis. This means students attend virtual classrooms from any location **online** through the Internet. Distance education/learning allows adults to earn college credits and even **entire** degrees usually from home or another **convenient** location off campus. These courses usually provide the same quality of instruction and cover the same material as traditional on-campus classes. The big differences are location and the use of technology, such as email, Internet, and CDs for instruction.

A **broader** definition of distance education/learning includes **non-degree** classes, such as non-credit courses, workshops, seminars, and career credits. People take these classes to learn a new skill or perhaps just pick up some new ideas for the fun of learning.

How a Distance Education Class Works

Instructors **post** assignments, syllabi, and course outlines on the Internet using specific **applications**. These programs allow the use of several communication **tools**, such as **discussion boards**, **chat rooms**, and email. Through these tools students interact with their instructors and classmates either in **real time** or at different times of the day.

Learning materials vary from class to class. Many include textbooks, video demonstrations, PowerPoint presentations, interactive lessons, and Web **resources**.

Learning activities may include writing papers, posting comments or essays to online discussion **forums**, completing individual or group projects, and taking quizzes/tests. Students can choose when and where they work. However, there are usually **deadlines** for homework and exams.

Types of Distance Education Classes

For some distance education courses, students never attend any on-campus classes. In these cases, they do all of the work **independently** through the computer and the Internet. Because these students never meet as a class, they interact with the instructor and classmates only through the use of technology.

For other distance education courses, students attend on-campus class sessions several times a semester and complete the **remaining** course work independently through the computer and Internet. This is a *blended* (or *hybrid*) class, and this kind of instruction allows the student to learn from both methods of teaching: online and **face-to-face**. In other words, students can interact with their instructor and classmates both in person during on-campus meetings and online through discussion forums, email, chat sessions, and *blogs*. These kinds of classes may have different rules and requirements at different schools. Therefore, students should check carefully about the details before they sign up for this type of class.

online diaries
(Web logs)

Comprehension Check

A. Main Ideas   Circle the letter of your answer.

In general this reading is about
a. the popularity of modern equipment/machines, such as cell phones and computers.

b. using computers and the Internet for classes.

c. using computers for both school and work.

B. Details

1. Put a check next to each statement that correctly describes distance learning/education.

_____ a. Distance learning requires the use of computers and the Internet.

_____ b. Students in every distance learning class must come to school at least a few times.

_____ c. Students in some distance learning classes do all their work at home and never come to school.

_____ d. Students taking distance education always plan to use those classes for a college degree.

_____ e. Students in these classes learn very different information than students taking the same classes in traditional classrooms.

_____ f. Students in these classes can never interact with each other.

_____ g. Students in these classes may never meet each other in a classroom, but they can have interaction through the computer.

2. Mark each of the characteristics of the course below in the space provided as follows:

- Write **D** if the characteristic describes a *distance learning* course.

- Write **T** if the characteristic describes a *traditional* course.

- Write **B** if the characteristic describes *both a distance learning and a traditional* course.

_____ a. It requires computers and the Internet all the time or almost all the time.

_____ b. It requires meeting with everyone in the class in a specific room for each class session.

_____ c. It requires taking the class in a virtual classroom all or most of the time.

_____ d. Students may never meet the teacher or other students in person.

_____ e. Students can take these classes for a degree.

_____ f. Students use textbooks.

_____ g. Students communicate with each other and with the teacher.

_____ h. Students take tests and quizzes.

_____ i. Teachers assign papers and other assignments.

_____ j. Students almost always work by themselves.

_____ k. Students have due dates for all assignments and projects.

Vocabulary Study

A. *Below you will find an underlined vocabulary word from the reading in each sentence and four definitions or synonyms after that sentence. Circle the **two** choices that have the same meaning as the vocabulary word. Follow the example.*

1. During my vacation I could not check my email because I did not have <u>access</u> to the Internet.

   (a.) an ability to make use of   b. a paid account

   (c.) a way to approach or get admittance   d. money to pay for

2. Sometimes you need a <u>broad</u> definition or explanation of something to fully understand it.

   a. small   b. wide

   c. general   d. unusual

3. Email is a very <u>convenient</u> way of communicating with people from computers at any location.

   a. cheap

   b. comfortable

   c. complicated

   d. handy/easy to use

4. The <u>entire</u> class failed the quiz, so the instructor gave another one the next week.

   a. part of

   b. small

   c. complete/total

   d. whole

5. Taking an online course usually requires the student to work <u>independently</u>.

   a. not subject to control of others

   b. under the supervision of others

   c. slowly and carefully

   d. separately/self governing

6. <u>Devices</u>, such as cell phones, make communication from any location easy.

   a. gifts

   b. inventions/mechanisms

   c. machines

   d. furniture

B. *Choose a definition/synonym from the following list for each of the underlined vocabulary words in the sentences. Write the letter of the answer on the line next to the sentence. The first one has been done as an example.*

   a. due date/time limit

   b. announce/publicize

   c. something used to work with

   d. leftover

   e. ~~machines that help with comfort~~

   f. source of information/support

   g. pastime/amusement

   h. not part of an academic degree

   _e_ 1. In some places the average person has many conveniences in his/her home such as phones, computers, and kitchen appliances.

   ____ 2. The instructor was absent from class, so she asked the secretary to <u>post</u> the homework assignment on the door of the classroom.

   ____ 3. Matt stayed up all night so he could meet the <u>deadline</u> to hand in his big report to the instructor.

   ____ 4. Many schools offer <u>non-degree</u> courses because some people want to take classes without a formal program.

____ 5. It is important for students to study hard but also to spend time on <u>recreation</u> sometimes.

____ 6. The instructor finished the lesson early, and then she used the <u>remaining</u> time for review.

____ 7. The library and the Internet are two <u>resources</u> for information.

____ 8. In the past people used typewriters as writing <u>tools</u>, but today most people use computers.

C. *In the reading you can find several words that relate to computers, the Internet, and distance learning. Look at the lists of words and meanings below and decide which meanings fit each word. In some cases one meaning may fit more than one word.*

Words
___ 1. applications ___ 2. chat rooms ___ 3. online ___ 4. real time
___ 5. face-to-face ___ 6. forums ___ 7. discussion boards

Meanings
a. connected to a computer network or communication system

d. open discussion or expression of ideas not necessarily all at the same time

b. online interactive discussion where everyone participates at the same time.

e. computer programs

c. actual time something takes place on the computer

f. in direct contact with each person at the same place

Discussion/Writing

Your teacher will tell you to answer these questions in writing or through discussion.

1. What did you think of your results of the questions in Part 1 (Preview) of this unit? Did these results surprise you in any way? Explain your answer.

2. Have you ever taken a distance education course? If so, describe this experience. If not, do you think you might like to take this kind of class? Why or why not?

PART 3   WRITING SENTENCES—SENTENCE COMBINING WITH SUBORDINATING CONJUNCTIONS

Read the paragraph about technology in the classroom and answer the questions that follow.

[1]In many schools today teachers use different kinds of technology in their classrooms during their lessons to improve their students' learning experiences. [2]They often use these teaching tools because they want to make their lessons more interactive. [3]In other words, if teachers want to increase student involvement during class time, they may use computers or other kinds of technology in their lessons. [4]Students may work on their own using these tools, or they may interact with other students in pairs or small groups on projects or assignments. [5]In addition, many teachers use technology because they want their students to become more independent learners. [6]For example students can find information on their own if they use computers to help them. [7]Therefore, these students may not simply memorize things, and they can become active, independent learners. [8]If instructors want to add variety to their lessons, they may make presentations with certain kinds of applications, such as PowerPoint. [9]For instance, they can present information using graphics, videos, and animation, so their lessons can become more interesting and alive for their students. [10]Because many people recognize student interest and involvement as keys to learning, some instructors use technology as an important tool for classroom instruction.

Reading

Technology in the Classroom

Questions

1. How many subject-verb combinations (clauses) do you see in Sentence 4 and Sentence 7 of the reading? (See Unit Three Part 3 for a review of clauses.) What word is putting the clauses together in each of these sentences?

2. a. Sentence 2 also has two clauses. Underline each clause. What word is putting these two clauses together? Circle that word.
   b. Underline the two clauses in sentence 6. Circle the word that is putting these clauses together.
   c. What punctuation do you see with two words you circled in these sentences?

3. Sentences 8 and 10 also each have two clauses. Underline the two clauses in each of these sentences. Circle the word that is putting the clauses together in each of these sentences. What punctuation do you see in each of these sentences?

4. On the lines below write the words you circled for questions 2 and 3. Write one word on each line.

   _____   _____

Explanation—Combining Sentences with Subordinating Conjunctions

1. In Unit Three you learned about putting sentences together with the coordinating conjunctions *and, but, so,* and *or.* When we use these connectors, or signals, we follow this pattern:

   _____, _____ _____
   sentence (clause) #1 comma   conjunction   sentence (clause) #2

   Students may work on their own using these tools, **or** they may interact with other students in pairs or small groups on projects or assignments.
   We call these two clauses *independent clauses* because each clause can stand on its own and be a complete sentence.

2. Another group of connectors/signals is called **subordinating conjunctions**. There are many subordinating conjunctions in English. Each one has a specific meaning and shows a relationship between the second clause and the first one. In this unit you will practice using two subordinating conjunctions as follows:

   a. Conjunction showing reason: *because*

      EXAMPLE: They often use these teaching tools **because**
                             sentence/clause #1
                  they want to make their lessons more interactive.
                             sentence/clause #2 (reason)

   b. Conjunction showing condition (something happens or will happen under this condition): *if*

      EXAMPLE: Students can find information on their own **if**
                             sentence/clause #1
                  they use computers to help them.
                             sentence/clause #2 (condition)

3. A subordinating conjunction can be in the middle of a sentence or at the beginning of a sentence. Look at the following two patterns.

   Pattern 1

   Place the conjunction between the two clauses (in the middle of the sentence).

   _____ _____ _____
   sentence/clause #1   subordinating conjunction   sentence/clause #2

      EXAMPLE: Students can find and use information on their own **if**
                             sentence/clause #1
                  they use computers to help them.
                             sentence/clause #2

EXAMPLE: They often use these teaching tools **because**
sentence/clause #1

they want to make their lessons more interactive.
sentence/clause #2

Pattern 2

Place the conjunction at the beginning of the sentence.

_____   _____   _____
subordinating conjunction   sentence/clause #1   sentence/clause #2

EXAMPLE: **If** students use computers to help them,
sentence/clause #1

they can find information on their own.
sentence/clause #2

EXAMPLE: **Because** they want to make their lessons more
sentence/clause #1

interactive, they often use these teaching tools.
sentence/clause #2

4. Punctuation and capitalization with subordinating conjunctions

a. As you learned in Unit Three with coordinating conjunctions, only the first word of the sentence should have a capital letter. Do not use a capital letter in the middle of the sentence.

INCORRECT: They often use these teaching tools because They want to make their lessons more interactive.

CORRECT: They often use these teaching tools because they want to make their lessons more interactive.

b. When we place subordinating conjunctions in between two clauses, we do not add a comma. This is because the subordinating conjunction is in between the two sentences or clauses. The end of the first sentence/clause and the beginning of the second sentence/clause are very clear.

EXAMPLE: Students can find and use information on their own **if**
sentence/clause #1

they use computers to help them.
sentence/clause #2

c. When we begin a sentence with a subordinating clause, we add a comma in between the two clauses to separate the two pieces of the sentence. In this way, the reader knows exactly where the first sentence/clause ends and the second sentence/clause begins.

EXAMPLE: **If** students use computers to help them,
sentence/clause #1   comma

they can find information on their own.
sentence/clause #2

5. Coordinating conjunctions combine two independent clauses. However, subordinating conjunctions combine two different types of clauses: *independent* and *dependent.* Dependent means it is not complete. In other words, it needs more information and does not make sense on its own.

Look at the following examples of dependent and independent clauses. Which ones can you understand without other information? (Which ones make sense by themselves?)

a. Students can find information on their own.

b. If they use computers to help them.

c. Because they want to make their lessons more interactive.

d. They often use these teaching tools.

Only sentences *a* and *d* are independent clauses and make sense. Sentences *b* and *c* are dependent clauses. We need more information to go with them in order to completely understand them. Dependent clauses are not complete sentences by themselves. If a clause begins with a subordinating conjunction, it is a dependent clause.

NOTE: Sometimes you will see these clauses with different names:

independent clause =   dependent clause =
main clause   *subordinate clause*

These names have the same meaning.

Editing Focus

Fragments,
Run-ons,
Comma Splices

6. **IMPORTANT—Errors to Avoid**

a. **Fragments** As explained above, dependent clauses need more information and are incomplete by themselves. Therefore, a dependent clause by itself is a mistake. It is a *fragment* because it is part of a sentence but not a complete sentence.

When you use subordinating conjunctions, you must be sure to have an independent clause in the sentence in addition to the dependent clause.

INCORRECT: Because they want to make their lessons more interactive.
fragment (dependent clause by itself)

CORRECT: Teachers often use these teaching tools because they want to make their lessons more interactive.

Because teachers want to make their lessons more interactive, they often use these teaching tools.

NOTE: Be careful about using *because* at the beginning of a sentence. In conversation, people may answer questions by starting with the word *because* and giving their answer as a fragment. In writing, this is not acceptable. Be sure you always include an independent clause after a dependent clause beginning with *because.*

EXAMPLE: Why do teachers use technology in the classroom?

Because they want to make their lessons more interactive. (conversation only—fragment in writing)

Because teachers want to make their lessons more interactive, they may use technology in their classroom.

b. *Run-on sentences*   Do not combine sentences without a signal or connector, such as a subordinating conjunction. Doing this will make a *run-on* sentence. A run-on sentence is not acceptable in written English.

run on

INCORRECT: Students can find and use information on their own they
subject   verb   subject
use computers to help them.
verb

CORRECT: Students can find and use information on their own if they
use computers to help them.

c. *Comma splices*   Do not connect clauses with just a comma and no other signal. A comma by itself is not an acceptable signal or connector. Putting a comma by itself between two clauses will make a *comma splice*. A comma splice is not acceptable in written English.

comma splice

INCORRECT: Students can find and use information on their own, they
subject   verb   subject
use computers to help them.
verb

CORRECT: Students can find and use information on their own if they use computers to help them.

NOTE: As discussed in Unit Three about coordinating conjunctions, you can also correct run-ons and comma splices by making separate sentences without a conjunction.

EXAMPLE: Students can find and use information on their own. They use computers to help them.

This is grammatically correct, and sometimes you may want to write two simple sentences. However, it's a good idea to try to have variety in your sentences as well. This means sometimes you should write simple sentences, and other times your sentences should be longer using connectors, such as subordinating conjunctions.

Practice: Sentence Combining—Using Subordinating Conjunctions **(because/if)**

A. Identifying Clauses and Subordinating Conjunctions
Put one line under each independent clause and two lines under each dependent clause in the sentences below. Then circle each subordinating conjunction. Follow the example.

1. *If a class is in a traditional classroom,*
   the instructor may use a computer in several ways.

2. In some schools many classrooms include computers as standard equipment because many teachers want to use them in their lessons.

3. If a classroom does not have a computer in the room, the teacher may get a portable "smart cart" to use in his/her class.

4. Some instructors use a computer because they want to show slide presentations with applications, such as PowerPoint.

5. Other instructors show students information from the World Wide Web if there is a computer available for the class.

6. Because Websites and applications, such as PowerPoint can present information through videos and animations, they can make lessons more interesting or easy to understand.

B. ***Matching Clauses***   *Match the clause in column A with the subordinating conjunction and clause that best fits from B. Use each answer only one time.*

A	B
1. Because computers allow students to do work at any time and location,	a. because they can be easy to give and score quickly.
2. Some instructors also assign computer tests and quizzes	b. s/he may require students to submit them electronically.
3. If an instructor assigns papers or projects,	c. if they feel comfortable using them.
4. Because some instructors read assignments online,	d. some instructors give assignments using them.
5. Some students may also make reports and presentations using applications like PowerPoint	e. they will give comments electronically as well.

C. *Combining Sentences*

1. Combine each pair of sentences below using the subordinating conjunction in parentheses. Place the conjunction either in the middle of your sentence or at the beginning according to the instructions in parentheses. Be sure to use correct punctuation for each sentence. Follow the examples.

   EXAMPLES: (*because* - middle)

   Many instructors post the syllabus and assignments on the Web.

   They want students to have access to that information at any time.

> *Many instructors post the syllabus and assignments on the*
> *Web because they want students to have access to that*
> *information at any time.*

EXAMPLE: (*because*—beginning)
Many instructors want students to have access to the syllabus and assignments at any time.

They post that information on the Web.

> *Because many instructors want students to have access to*
> *the syllabus and assignments at any time, they post that*
> *information on the Web.*

a. (*because* - beginning)

Some instructors want students to be responsible for all the information in the class.

They post their lectures and other class materials on the Web.

_____

_____

b. (*because* - middle)

Some instructors post their lectures and other class materials on the Web.

They want students to be responsible for all the information in the class.

_____

_____

c. (*if* - beginning)

A student is absent from class.

S/he can still get the missed materials at any time of the day on the Internet.

_____

_____

d. (*if* - middle)

A student can get the missed materials at any time of the day on the Internet.

S/he is absent from class.

_____

_____

e. (*if* - beginning)

Students want to get full credit or extra credit in the course.

They often must participate in discussions and chats online.

_____

_____

f. (*because* - middle)

Students must often participate in discussions and chats online.

The instructor requires these activities for full credit.

_____

_____

2. Combine each pair of sentences about computer labs using either *because* or *if*. In some cases both conjunctions may be correct, but you should choose only one for each of your answers. For some of your sentences, use the conjunction at the beginning of the sentence. For other answers, place the conjunction in the middle of the sentence. Be sure your sentences make sense with the order of the clauses. Use correct punctuation for each sentence. Follow the example.

EXAMPLE: Many schools have computer labs.

Instructors want students to be able to practice their skills outside the classroom.

Many schools have computer labs because instructors want students to be able to practice their skills outside the classroom. OR

Because instructors want students to be able to practice their skills outside the classroom, many schools have computer labs.

a. An instructor wants students to have extra practice in a subject (such as reading or math).

The students can go to the computer lab to do this.

_____

_____

b. Most instructors require neatly typed assignments.

Students may also want to use computer labs for reports and papers.

_____

_____

c. Some students don't have access to the Internet at home.

They may use computer labs at school to find information on the Web for their assignments.

_____

_____

d. Sometimes students may use computer labs at school to type their papers and assignments.

It is more convenient for their schedules.

_____

e. Textbooks offer extra practice or tests and quizzes on a Website. Instructors may require their students to complete these.

_____

_____

f. Some instructors may tell students to go to these Websites. They want to receive extra credit in addition to the extra practice.

_____

_____

D. ***Completing Sentences on Your Own***   *Review the reading in Part 2 (pages 122–123). Complete the following sentences with information you learned from this reading. Be sure to use your own words in your answers and include correct punctuation. Follow the example.*

EXAMPLE: If a student feels comfortable using computers, <u>s/he may want to take an online class.</u>

1. Because distance learning classes take place in virtual classrooms

_____

2. Some students take online classes because

_____

3. Other people do not take classes online because

_____

4. Students may meet for an online class in a regular classroom several times during the semester if

_____

5. If a student wants a flexible schedule to do work for a class

_____

6. Because online classes allow students to earn credits through computer work

_____

7. Students in online classes can interact with their classmates because

_____

8. In distance education if an instructor wants to give a test

_____

E. ***Finding Sentence Problems***   *In all of the sentences below you will find more information about online classes and advice for success in these classes. Follow the directions for correcting the problems in each sentence.*

1. ***Fragments***—Put a line under each fragment. Then show how to fix the problem. Do not change any of the words or information in the sentences. Follow the example.

EXAMPLE: If you want to be successful in an online class~~x~~ ,

~~y~~You should be comfortable with and understand the computer application for the course.

a. You should make sure you can easily use discussion boards and chats. If you want to succeed in the class.

b. You should also be sure to participate in online conferencing. Because it is important to interact with other students in the course.

c. If you want to participate fully. You should try to give your ideas and read your classmates' comments as much as possible.

d. Because your classmates may be able to help you learn. You should not interact with the teacher only.

2. *Run-ons*—Each sentence below is a run-on. Correct each one in two ways:

• Show how to make two separate sentences/clauses.

• Combine the two clauses into one good sentence using the conjunction given. Be sure to use correct punctuation in all of your answers. Follow the example.

EXAMPLE: You should try to establish a support system with friends and family. you may need to work around them at home on weekends or at night.

(because) You should try to establish a support system with friends and family because you may need to work around them at home on weekends or at night.

OR Because you may need to work around family and friends at home on weekends or at night, you should try to establish a support system with them.

a. Students have a private study space they will be more successful.

(if) _____

_____

b. Students should not try to share study space with other people they may not have enough time to do all the work for the class.

(because) _____

_____

c. You should check your online course almost every day you need to keep track of other people's comments and all the assigned work.

(because) _____

_____

d. Some students don't check online regularly they may not be able to catch up on all the work.

(if) _____

_____

3. *Comma splices*—Each sentence below is a comma splice. Correct each one in two ways:

- Show how to make two separate sentences/clauses.

- Combine the two clauses into one good sentence using the conjunction given. Be sure to use correct punctuation in all of your answers.

a. Some people feel nervous about speaking in class, they might feel more comfortable using the computer to give their comments.

(if) _____

_____

b. Some students might be comfortable with online participation, they can think carefully about their comments before typing them.

(because) _____

_____

c. Online communication involves words without seeing other people, some people may forget to be polite and respectful.

(because) _____

_____

d. It is important to always be polite and respectful of other students, you take an online class.

(if) _____

_____

4. In the following paragraph find the following mistakes:

- one fragment

- one run-on

- one comma splice

- two incorrect commas (not comma splices)

Show how to correct these mistakes. In some cases you may need to add *because* or *if* to a sentence to make your correction.

Tips for Taking Online Classes

Because an online class requires students to work independently. Some people may forget about asking for help. Students should work cooperatively with other students to find answers, if they need help in an online class. Students must say something to get help they have technical difficulties or problems understanding something. Students must communicate their need for help, because other students and the teacher won't know about this need in an online class. Students take an online class, they sometimes must think a little differently about communication.

Discussion/Writing

Your teacher will tell you to answer these questions in writing or through discussion.

1. How much technology do your instructors use in the classroom? Do your classes include any of the kinds of computer activities mentioned in the exercises in Part 3? What do you think about using these kinds of activities in your classes?

2. Does your school have a computer lab? If so, how often do you use it and what kinds of things do you do there? What do you think about using this lab?

PART 4 WRITING PARAGRAPHS—SUPPORTING SENTENCES—OPINIONS AND REASONS

Read the paragraph about distance learning and then answer the questions that follow.

Distance Learning: An Excellent Educational Experience

Last semester I took an online history course, and now I am fully in support of this kind of learning. This course was perfect for me because it allowed me to do the work around my usual schedule. Because I work at least 30 hours a week, it is difficult for me to get to school at a specific time for a class. In my online class I could be flexible and work at the times best for my schedule. In addition, in traditional classrooms I often feel left out of class discussions. In class I am a shy person, and I usually like to think about my answers carefully. However, in this class if I had something to contribute to a discussion board, I could easily participate from my home with more time to think. In fact, I also had more time to interact with my classmates online because in traditional classes I usually do not have time to discuss anything before or after class. Finally, my busy schedule also makes it difficult to see an instructor during office hours for questions or extra help. In the online class, I found the instructor very accessible through e-mail, and this was a big help to me. In conclusion, I was very happy with my online history class last semester, so I plan to take another online class in the near future.

Paragraph Discussion

1. Does this paragraph follow correct paragraph format? Does it have all of the following?

    ___ a title centered above the paragraph
    ___ correct capitalization of the title
    ___ indenting of the first sentence
    ___ each sentence following the one before
    ___ correct left and right margins
    ___ a capital letter at the beginning of each new sentence
    ___ end punctuation for each sentence

2. Which sentence in this paragraph is the topic sentence? What is the main idea of this paragraph?

3. What kind of information do the supporting sentences give?

4. Does this paragraph have a concluding sentence?

Writing Focus
Paragraph
Organization:
Supporting
Sentences—Giving
Opinions and
Reasons

Paragraph Organization: Supporting Sentences—Giving Opinions and Reasons

A. Giving Opinions In Unit Three you learned about using facts to provide specific details and support in a paragraph. Sometimes you may also write your opinions, and these are different from facts.

Facts: A fact is something that is always true. We can prove a fact.

EXAMPLES: Online classes require students to use computers.

Students in online classes need access to the Internet.

People can use laptop computers at many different locations.

Opinions: An opinion may be different from one person to another. It is not always true for everybody. Each of the following opinions may be true for some people but not for others.

EXAMPLES: Class discussions are important and helpful.

Online discussions are better than classroom discussions.

Using a computer for schoolwork is difficult.

Sometimes writers will use the following words to state an opinion:

- I think
- I believe
- I feel
- in my opinion
- I support (or do not support)

B. Providing Reasons

1. When you write an opinion, you should also include reasons to support this opinion.

Opinion: Class discussions are important and helpful.

Reasons: Discussions help me understand the readings.

It's good to know other people's ideas about a topic.

It gives me a chance to interact with my classmates.

2. Look back at the paragraph about online classes on page 139 and answer the following questions:

a. What opinion is the writer of the sample paragraph giving?

_____

b. Is it possible that someone else might have a different opinion about this subject? What might be a different opinion about this subject? _____

_____

c. What reasons does the writer give as support for this opinion?

_____

_____

_____

d. Does the writer give support for these reasons? In other words, does the writer explain these reasons? Put a line under the sentences that explain each reason in the paragraph on page 138.

_____

Practice: Identifying Facts and Opinions

A. Decide if each of the following is a fact or an opinion. Label each one as F for fact or O for opinion in the space given.

_____ 1. Many teachers use technology in the classroom.

_____ 2. Teachers should tell students everything in a face-to-face classroom.

_____ 3. Some teachers give Internet assignments to their students for homework.

_____ 4. Looking for information on the Internet does not help students learn.

_____ 5. Interactive lessons on the computer make learning easier.

_____ 6. Some instructors teach new information in their lessons with PowerPoint presentations.

B. Following each number below are two opinions and one fact. Circle the letter next to the fact in each group. Follow the example.

1. (a.) Assignments for an online class are posted on the Internet.

   b. Completing assignments on time for an online class is easy.

   c. Instructions for online assignments are difficult to understand.

2. a. It is important for a student to feel a like s/he is a part of a class.

   b. Using a computer to contact people in the class is not comfortable.

   c. Interaction with classmates takes place through discussion boards and e-mail in online classes.

3. a. A hybrid class is better than other online classes.

   b. A hybrid class includes both online and face-to-face instruction.

   c. A hybrid class is very convenient.

Practice: Paragraph Organization

These days some college and university classes require students to bring lap-top computers to the classroom. However, some instructors do not want their students to have these computers in their classes. Read the following paragraph and then follow the instructions for the activity after it.

Writing Focus

Paragraph Organization: Topic Sentence, Opinions and Reasons, Conclusions

No Laptops in the Classroom

Bringing laptop computers into my classroom is a bad idea for several reasons. First of all, I don't like those computers in the classroom because they do not allow students to be fully involved in my class. For example, many students try to type almost every word I say, so they are spending almost all their class time typing. If they spend so much time typing, they do not have time to think about the information. In addition, I think computers can create a rude environment. Students may never look up at classmates or me because they are typing all the time. There may be no eye contact at all during the class, and for an instructor that is not polite. Also, the constant noise of tapping on computer keys can bother some people. Furthermore, some students start to lose attention in the class, so they turn their attention to their computers. For example, they may use their laptops to email friends or even do work for other classes during my class time. Finally, some students use their laptops to help them cheat on quizzes and exams. It is difficult for teachers to check each student for this. For all of these reasons, I do not like laptop computers in my classroom, and I will not allow students to bring them to my class.

A. Answer the questions about the writer's opinions.

1. What is the writer's opinion about bringing laptop computers into the classroom? Is this writer for or against laptops in the classroom?

2. Underline the topic sentence.

3. How many reasons does the writer give for her opinion about laptop computers in the classroom? List these reasons.

_____

_____

_____

_____

4. Underline the sentences in the paragraph that support each reason you listed in 3.

5. Circle the concluding sentence.

B.   Look at the following information for a paragraph about use of laptop computers in the classroom. The writer of this paragraph has a different opinion than the writer of the paragraph above. This writer believes laptops in the classroom can help students learn. Do the following for this activity:

1. Read the list of reasons. Do all of them fit the topic of this paragraph? If not, cross out the ones that do not fit.

2. Write a topic sentence for this paragraph.

3. Write a concluding sentence for this paragraph.

Title: Laptop Computers in the Classroom

Topic Sentence: _____

_____

Reasons:

1. provide many opportunities for student participation

2. students find information on their own on the Internet

3. students can see real life experiences and illustrations of ideas and theories

4. students may not pay attention to the teacher and may email their friends

5. students can get most up-to-date information and can go beyond their textbook's information

6. instructors can work more closely with individual students while others are working

Conclusion: _____

_____

Discussion/Writing

Your teacher will tell you to answer these questions in writing or through discussion.

1. What is your opinion about students using laptop computers in the classroom? Which of the writers above do you agree with? Explain your answer. Would you like to use a laptop in the classroom? Why or why not?

2. How much do you use computers and the Internet for school? Are you comfortable using computers for homework and other assignments for your classes? Explain your answers.

Writing Assignment

Picking the Topic

Choose one of the following questions and write a paragraph. Be sure to include a topic sentence with your opinion, reasons for this opinion, support for your reasons, and a concluding sentence.

1. What is your opinion about teachers using technology in the classroom? Do you think this is a good way to teach and to learn? Explain why you feel this way.

2. What is your opinion about teachers requiring students to use computers and the Internet for homework and assignments? Do you think it is a good idea or a bad idea to require students to do this in the classroom or outside the classroom? Explain why you feel this way.

Following the Steps in the Writing Process

Before You Write

■ *Step One: Thinking about the Topic/Getting ideas*
First, think about the writing assignments above. What ideas do you have for each topic? Write as many ideas as you can in the spaces below. Try to think of as many reasons as possible for your opinion. You do not need to write complete sentences and don't worry about organization for this part.

Teachers Using Technology—a good idea

Teachers Using Technology—not a good idea

Using Computers for Homework and Assignments—a good idea

Using Computers for Homework and Assignments—not a good idea

Now choose one of these topics to write your paragraph about.

■ *Step Two: Organizing Your Thoughts and Ideas*
Think about the main idea of your paragraph.

Topic Sentence

   a. What is your topic? Will you write about teachers or students using technology for classes?

   Topic: _____

   b. What is your controlling idea? What opinion are you giving about this topic?

   Controlling idea: _____

   c. Write your topic sentence on the chart at the end of this unit (page 148).

Support

   d. Look back at your notes for Step One and circle the reasons you want to include. Make sure your paragraph has enough reasons and explanation of those reasons.

   e. Write your ideas for support on the chart at the end of this unit (page 148). You do not need to write complete sentences on this chart, but you should include specific words from the chart in Step One on pages 144–145.

Concluding Sentence

   f. Write a concluding sentence. Remember to restate the main idea of the paragraph or topic sentence or give a summary of the paragraph. Write this sentence on the chart on page 148.

   g. Write a title for this paragraph on the chart at the end of this unit (page 148).

■ *Step Three: Getting Feedback about the Chart*
Show your chart to another person. Your teacher may ask you to work with a partner and complete a review of your chart/outline. Use the review sheet on page 201 in the Appendix for this feedback.

When You Write

■ *Step Four: Writing the First Draft (Rough Draft)*
Write your first draft of the paragraph. Do not worry about perfect grammar, spelling, punctuation, or capitalization for this draft. Make sure you write this first draft using the ideas on the chart/outline (page 148).

Be sure to include the following in your rough draft:

• Make a title.

• Begin the paragraph with a topic sentence.

• Support your topic sentence with reasons and explanations of those reasons.

• Make sure you have enough support (at least five to seven sentences).

• Use coordinating conjunctions and the two subordinating conjunctions from this lesson,

• Use at least three vocabulary words from this unit.

• End your paragraph with a concluding sentence. (Restate the main idea or give a summary of the paragraph in this sentence.)

After You Write

Check Your Work
After you finish writing the first draft, read your paragraph again. Check your work for the following. Do this before you show it to anyone else.

☐ This paragraph discusses one of the following:

• why I think teachers should use technology in the classroom

• why I think teachers should not use technology in the classroom

• why I think requiring students to use computers for assignments is a good idea

• why I think requiring students to use computers for assignments is not a good idea

☐ This paragraph has a title.

☐ This paragraph has a topic sentence.

☐ This paragraph has at least five to seven sentences of support/details.

☐ All of the details are reasons and support for those reasons.

☐ All of my reasons support the topic sentence.

☐ This paragraph has a concluding sentence.

☐ I used three vocabulary words from this lesson in the paragraph.

☐ I wrote some simple sentences and some sentences with coordinating conjunctions.

☐ I used the subordinating conjunctions *because* and *if* in some sentences.

☐ I checked each sentence for fragments (missing subjects or verbs or dependent clauses by themselves).

☐ I checked each sentence for run-ons and comma splices.

This paragraph has the correct paragraph form as follows:

☐ The title is centered above the paragraph.

☐ The title has correct capitalization.

☐ The title does not end in a period.

☐ I indented the first sentence of the paragraph.

☐ I have correct margins on the left and right.

☐ I did not put punctuation (period, comma, question mark) at the beginning of a new line.

☐ I double-spaced (skipped a space after every line).

☐ All of my sentences follow one another. (I did not go to the next line with a new sentence.)

■ *Step Five: Getting Feedback about the First Draft*
Show someone your first draft of the paragraph. Your teacher will decide the type of feedback you will receive for the first draft. It may be with a partner or from the teacher or both ways. For review with a partner, use the sheets on pages 202–203 in the Appendix.

■ *Step Six: Making Changes*
After you receive feedback, make some changes. First, decide if you want to change your topic sentence. Then decide if you want to change your supporting sentences by adding new ones or taking out some. Decide if you want to change your concluding sentence. After you make these changes, look at all the grammar, punctuation, spelling, and capitalization. Make any necessary changes in these things as well.

■ *Step Seven: The Final Draft*
Type your final draft on a computer. Try to make this paragraph as perfect as you can.

Organizing Your Thoughts for Writing

TITLE: _____

TOPIC SENTENCE

Reason: Support for reason:	Reason: Support for reason:
Reason: Support for reason:	Reason: Support for reason:
Reason: Support for reason:	Reason: Support for reason:

SUPPORT

SUPPORT

CONCLUDING SENTENCE

_____
_____
_____

Myths/Fables/ Legends/Folk Stories

Content Area: Cross-Cultural Stories/Literature

Reading: Traditional Storytelling

Short Readings: The Beginning of Earth and People
Pandora's Box
A Thousand and One Nights
The Milkmaid and Her Pail
Pecos Bill and the Tornado
The Fox and the Grapes
How the World Burst from an Egg
The Woman Who Fell from the Sky

Sentence Writing Focus: Combining Sentences with Subordinating
Conjunctions of Time (*before/after/when/ while/as/until*)

Editing Focus: Run-ons/Comma Splices/Fragments

Writing Focus: Paragraphs (Narration/Storytelling/Chronology)
Supporting Sentences

PART 1   UNIT PREVIEW

Preview Activity: What Stories Do You Know?

A. *What do you know about some of the different types of traditional stories? Can you explain the differences between each of the following? Can you give an example of each one?*

1. a myth _____

2. a legend _____

3. a fable _____

4. a folk story (folktale) _____

B. *Match the information in Column B with the story it goes with in Column A. Write the letter of your answer on each line next to the numbers.*

A	B
____ 1. ancient Greek and Roman god names	a. Phan Ku
____ 2. Aesop's fable	b. Kwaku Ananse
____ 3. 1,001 Arabian Nights	c. Paul Bunyan and Babe
____ 4. Chinese story of the beginning of the world	d. Zeus/Jupiter
____ 5. African spider tales	e. Scheherazade
____ 6. tall tales of the United States	f. The Fox and the Grapes

What do you know about these stories and characters? What other traditional stories do you know? Discuss your answers with your group and the class as a whole.

Quickwrite/Freewrite

Write for five minutes about the following topic. Do not worry about grammar, spelling, or punctuation. Just write what comes to your mind about the topic.

• What was your favorite story when you were a child? What was it about and why was it your favorite?

PART 2   READING AND VOCABULARY

People have been telling stories about life and the world around them for thousands of years. Many of these stories have **survived** through **oral** traditions, but others have been in writing for many years. There are several types of traditional **tales** and many reasons for telling them. Some explain the physical world around us, and others give lessons about life. The different types of stories have different names, including *myths*, *legends*, *fables*, and *folk stories* or *folktales*.

Myths are ancient stories that typically try to explain natural **occurrences** or practices and beliefs of a culture or society. These stories may include supernatural beings, gods, ancestors from the **remote** past, and **heroes**. Myths often discuss matters of great importance, such as the **creation** of the world, the first people, and the **origin** of fire. People define the world as they experience it, and their myths explain what they see. Therefore, the same natural occurrence may have a large variety of mythical explanations. For example, in Norse Viking stories the world

began when fire from the south met ice from the north. In an ancient Chinese story, the world began when a giant exploded from an egg.

Legends are also traditional stories about human heroes. However, they come from a different time period than myths because they are tales from the more recent past. They do not have clear historical **evidence**, but many people accept them as true or based on some facts. As generation after generation of storytellers told legends through the years, they added details and characters to make their stories more interesting. By adding more and more heroic and **thrilling** information, the storytellers made sure people wanted to continue to hear or read them. Examples of these kinds of stories are the *Iliad* and the *Odyssey*. These stories were old when the Greek poet Homer began to tell them, and we continue to read the written **versions** of them today.

Fables are **fictitious** stories that include a **moral** or message to the listener or reader. Often in fables animals, plants, and other forces of nature speak and act like humans, and there may be supernatural occurrences in these stories. Through these tales the storyteller communicates a useful lesson or some wisdom about life. Often these stories try to help us understand people's character and behavior through their strengths and weaknesses. Two famous fable storytellers were an ancient Greek named Aesop and a Frenchman named La Fontaine, but these kinds of stories exist in many cultures around the world.

Folk stories (folktales) are also fiction and often show how people **cope** with the world around them. They are usually **anonymous** stories that people **circulate** through the years. These tales may be about rich people or poor folk, and may include animals that speak out like people. Many of the world's folktales **resemble** each other in several ways, such as similar characters and **plots**. People remember and share these stories because they discuss timeless and placeless human situations in exciting and interesting ways. One popular kind of folk story in the United States is the *tall tale*. These are **humorous** stories of **exaggerated** characters, who have superhuman strength and abilities. Some well-known tall tales are about a giant lumberjack named Paul Bunyan and his blue ox named Babe, and others are about a rough and wild cowboy named Pecos Bill.

Comprehension Check

A. Main Ideas
Circle the letter of your answer.

1. This reading mainly discusses

    a. why some stories are the same all over the world.

    b. how storytelling changed from oral stories to written ones.

    c. several kinds of traditional stories.

2. Match each kind of story with its definition. Write the letter of your answer on the line.

A	B
____ 1. myth	a. a story about people from any time or place
____ 2. legend	b. a story that tries to explain people or nature
____ 3. fable	c. a story based on some truth but with added pieces
____ 4. folk story	d. a story with a message

B. Details
Below you will find a list of characteristics of the traditional stories discussed in the reading. Some of these are the same for the different kinds of stories, and some may be typical of only one kind of story. Write the numbers of the characteristics in the correct column(s) on the chart. You should write the number of the characteristic in as many columns as it applies. Follow the example.

1. stories about heroes

2. stories about supernatural beings or people with super strength

3. stories with animals that talk

4. stories that explain the origin of people or creation of the world

5. stories with some truth that changed over time to become more interesting

6. a story that teaches a lesson to be careful about something

7. a tall tale with exaggerated characters, such as a giant man

8. Aesop and La Fontaine

9. oral stories that became written

Myth	Legend	Fable	Folk story (Folktale)
1	1		

Vocabulary Study

A. Below you will find an underlined vocabulary word from the reading in each sentence and four definitions or synonyms after that sentence. Circle the two choices that have the same meaning as the vocabulary word. Follow the example.

1. Traditional stories may be <u>anonymous</u> because they are so old.

   (a.) nameless   b. very long

   (c.) no author's name   d. uninteresting

2. A story may begin in one place but <u>circulate</u> because it is so popular.

   a. change   b. pass from person to person

   c. become well known   d. become longer

3. Sometimes problems in life are difficult to <u>cope</u> with, so people tell stories about them.

   a. manage   b. overcome

   c. enjoy   d. remember

4. Some people like to tell <u>exaggerated</u> stories in order to make their actions seem more important.

   a. untrue   b. boring

   c. overstated   d. enlarged or increased beyond normal

5. People make take <u>fictitious</u> names for themselves because they don't want people to find them.

   a. long   b. not real

   c. imaginary   d. unusual

6. The <u>moral</u> of a story is usually the most important part of it.

   a. end   b. beginning

   c. principle of right or   d. important or practical lesson
      wrong behavior

7. Today in some cultures people continue to tell only <u>oral</u> stories just as they did in the past.

    a. spoken   b. unwritten

    c. without words   d. very old

8. If you live in a <u>remote</u> area, you may not get the most recent or up-to-date news.

    a. nearby   b. distant

    c. popular   d. separated or far removed

9. Some stories <u>survive</u> for hundreds or even thousands of years because they are so popular.

    a. continue to live or exist   b. go away

    c. remain alive   d. change

10. Two stories from different cultures may <u>resemble</u> each other because they have the same main ideas.

    a. be alike   b. be very different from

    c. be similar to   d. be boring

B. Choose a definition/synonym from the following list for each of the under-lined vocabulary words in the sentences. Write the letter of the answer on the line next to the sentence. The first one has been done as an example.

a. funny   f. event

b. person of great achievement   g. accounts/interpretations

c. exciting   h. stories

d. beginning   i. ~~bring something into existence~~

e. support/proof   j. main story/plan

__i__ 1. People <u>create</u> stories in order to try to explain the natural world around them.

_____ 2. Scientists sometimes find <u>evidence</u> that parts of a very old story might be true.

_____ 3. A <u>hero</u> of a story can be superhuman or can be an everyday person.

_____ 4. Many people prefer <u>humorous</u> stories because they like to laugh.

_____ 5. An unusual <u>occurrence</u> of stars or planets in the sky could make ancient people afraid.

_____ 6. Nobody knows the <u>origin</u> of some stories because they are so old.

_____ 7. Sometimes the <u>plot</u> of a book is complicated and difficult to follow.

_____ 8. Some <u>tales</u> may include animals or plants that talk.

____ 9. Listening to an old story late at night outside in the dark can be <u>thrilling</u>.

____ 10. Stories may travel through time, so different generations may tell different <u>versions</u> of the same tale.

Discussion/Writing

Your teacher will tell you to answer these questions in writing or through discussion.

1. What are the most popular traditional stories in your culture? Why do you think people enjoy listening to or reading about these stories?

2. What are your personal favorite kinds of traditional stories to listen to or to read in your native language? Do you read any of them in English? If you do not enjoy traditional stories, explain why not.

PART 3   WRITING SENTENCES—SENTENCE COMBINING—WITH SUBORDINATING CONJUNCTIONS OF TIME

Read the following story from the ancient Greeks and answer the questions that follow.

Reading
The Beginning of Earth and People

[1]Before the Earth existed, there was darkness. [2]While land, water, and air were *whirling* together, this created a mess called Chaos. [3]Land was almost liquid, water was almost solid, and air was a little bit of both. [4]As nature straightened it all out, this became our Earth. [5]Then came a race of giant gods called Titans. [6]One of these Titans, Prometheus, put dirt and water together until he made a man. [7]The man looked like Prometheus, but he was much smaller. [8]When Prometheus created this man, he allowed him to stand straight up in order to see the stars. [9]However, because this man did not have sharp *claws* or teeth or long legs (like some animals on earth), he couldn't protect himself. [10]Prometheus decided to do something when he realized this problem. [11]He lit a *torch* on the wheel of the sun's chariot, brought down fire from heaven, and gave it to man. [12]After man learned to use this fire, he was able to make metal weapons to protect himself. [13]He could also make tools to help him work the soil and grow food. [14]In addition, during the cold winter he could keep warm near a fire until the better weather came.

turning/spinning

animal nails

burning stick

Questions

1. How many clauses (subject-verb combinations) do you see in sentence 10 of the reading above? Underline each clause in sentence 10. What word is putting those sentences together? Circle that word.

2. Follow the same instructions you did for question 1 above for sentence 1, sentence 2, sentence 4, sentence 6, and sentence 12 in the reading.

3. On the lines below write each word you circled for questions 1 and 2. Write one word on each line.

_____   _____   _____   _____   _____   _____

Sentence-Combining Focus

Subordinating Conjunctions of Time (*before, after, until, while, when, as*)

Explanation: Combining Sentences with Subordinating Conjunctions of Time

1. In Unit Five you learned about combining sentences with two subordinating conjunctions: *because* and *if*. In this unit you will learn about several more subordinating conjunctions, and these words put sentences/clauses together showing a time relationship.

2. Review of Subordinating Conjunctions

a. A subordinating conjunction can be in the middle of a sentence or at the beginning of a sentence. There will be no comma if the subordinating conjunction is in the middle of the sentence. If the subordinating conjunction is at the beginning of the sentence, add a comma between the two clauses. Follow these patterns:

Pattern 1

Place the conjunction between the two clauses (in the middle of the sentence). Do not add a comma.

_____   _____   _____
sentence/clause #1   subordinating conjunction   sentence/clause #2

INCORRECT: The man could not protect himself, because he did not have sharp claws or teeth. (incorrect comma)

CORRECT: The man could not protect himself because he did not have sharp claws or teeth. (no comma needed)

Pattern 2

Place the conjunction at the beginning of the sentence. Add a comma between the two clauses.

_____   _____,   _____
subordinating conjunction   sentence/clause #1   sentence/clause #2

INCORRECT: Because the man did not have sharp claws or teeth he could not protect himself. (missing comma)

CORRECT: Because the man did not have sharp claws or teeth, he could not protect himself. (correct comma)

b. Use correct capitalization with these sentences.

INCORRECT: The man could not protect himself Because he did not have sharp teeth or claws.

CORRECT: The man could not protect himself because he did not have sharp teeth or claws.

c. Subordinating conjunctions connect two kinds of clauses: *independent* and *dependent*. The dependent clause in these sentences begins with a subordinating conjunction.

EXAMPLES:

This man could not protect himself because he did not have teeth or claws.
independent clause   subordinating   dependent
                                                conjunction   clause

Because this man did not have teeth or claws, he could not protect himself.
subordinating   dependent clause   independent clause
conjunction

3. Below are some subordinating conjunctions of time and examples of how they are used.

after = later than
After man learned to use this fire, he was able to make metal
          dependent clause   *independent clause*
weapons to protect himself.

before = earlier than
Before the Earth existed, there was darkness.
          dependent clause   *independent clause*

until = up to that time
One of these Titans, Prometheus, put dirt and water together
          independent clause
until he made a man.
          dependent clause

while = during that time
While land, water, and air were whirling together, this created a mess
          dependent clause   *independent clause*
called Chaos.

when = at that time
Prometheus decided to do something **when** he realized this problem.
          independent clause   *dependent clause*

as = at that time/when
As nature straightened it all out, this became our Earth.
          dependent clause   *independent clause*

NOTE: Clauses that follow *when, while,* and *as* often include past progressive verb forms.

6. **IMPORTANT—Errors to Avoid**

   a. **Fragments** A dependent clause by itself is a *fragment*.

   INCORRECT: When he realized this problem. (fragment)

   CORRECT: He decided to do something when he realized this problem. OR

   When he realized this problem, he decided to do something.

   b. **Run-ons** If you do not use a signal (connector), such as a subordinating conjunction to put clauses together, you will have a run-on.

   INCORRECT: Prometheus decided to do something he realized this problem.
   run-on

   CORRECT: Prometheus decided to do something when he realized this problem.

   c. **Comma Splices** If you use a comma in between clauses without any signal/connector, you will have a comma splice.

   INCORRECT: Prometheus decided to do something, he realized this
   comma splice
   problem.

   CORRECT: Prometheus decided to do something when he realized this problem.

7. **Before and After** *Before* and *after* may act as prepositions and as subordinating conjunctions. How can you know the difference?

   a. These words are subordinating conjunctions when they begin a dependent clause with at least a subject and a verb following them. Subordinating conjunctions combine two sentences/clauses.

   Before the Earth existed, there was darkness.
   conjunction S   V   S   V

   dependent clause   independent clause

   Man could make metal weapons to protect himself **after** he learned to use fire.
   S   V   conjunction S   V
   independent clause   dependent clause

   b. These words are prepositions when a noun follows them. In these cases they are not combining sentences/clauses.

   Before that time there was darkness.
   preposition noun   S   V

   Prometheus created man **after** that time.
   S   V   preposition   noun

Practice: Sentence Combining—Using Subordinating Conjunctions of Time

A. Identifying Clauses and Conjunctions

1. Underline each dependent clause starting with a subordinating conjunction in the following story. Circle each of those conjunctions. Follow the example in Sentence 1.

2. Find any coordinating conjunctions in these sentences. Circle each coordinating conjunction and underline the clause that follows it. Follow the example in Sentence 4.

PANDORA'S BOX

(After) <u>Prometheus stole fire from the sun</u>, Jupiter became angry with him. He made a plan to punish Prometheus for giving fire to humans. First, Jupiter told the gods and goddesses on Mount Olympus to create a beautiful woman to send to Earth. He named this woman Pandora, (and) <u>he gave her a box.</u> As he gave Pandora this box, he told her never to open it. Pandora agreed, and she went down to Earth to become a gift to Prometheus. However, Prometheus didn't trust Jupiter. Therefore, he wouldn't let Pandora in the door when she arrived. Then his brother, Epimetheus, asked Pandora to become his wife, so she moved right in. For a short time while Pandora was living with Epimetheus, she was enjoying her life on Earth. One day she became bored, and she thought about the box from Jupiter. She remembered his words, but she decided to open it anyway. Immediately as she opened the lid, devils and demons flew out from inside the box. Before she could stop them, they spread over the earth. Then they made everyone sick and miserable. Pandora felt terrible until she saw one thing still in the box. It was hope. When she saw hope in the box, she felt better. Hope is very important because the world cannot exist without it!

B. Fill in the blanks   *Fill in each blank space with one of the subordinating conjunctions of time: before, after, until, when, while, as. Some spaces may have more than one possible answer, but you should write only one conjunction in each space. Be sure to use each conjunction at least once.*

A Thousand and One Nights

Long ago a Sultan lived in his palace and ruled his land from there. _____ this Sultan Shahriyar was ruling, he made a cruel law. This law allowed him to marry many wives one after the other. First, he made a wedding with one wife. _____ they were married for one night, she had to be put to death the next morning. Many beautiful girls died in this way _____ a woman named Scheherazade at last offered to be the Sultan's bride. _____ she married the Sultan, she asked her sister to visit him on the morning following the wedding. Scheherazade wanted to tell the Sultan one story, and he agreed to this favor. _____ Scheherazade was telling her first story, the Sultan was very interested. Therefore, he decided she should live because he wanted her to finish the story. _____ Scheherazade was telling her story every night, she made sure to stop it at the most exciting part. In this way, she saved her life every night. The Sultan did not want to kill her _____ she could finish the story. _____ she continued to tell her stories for a thousand and one nights, the Sultan fell in love with her. Thus, the Sultan's cruel law did not continue _____ he married Scheherazade.

C. Combining Sentences   Combine the two sentences next to each number using the subordinating conjunction given in parentheses. Put the conjunction at the beginning of some sentences and in the middle of other sentences. Be sure to use correct punctuation. Follow the example.

EXAMPLE: (when) African storytellers talk about Kwaku Ananse ("spider man").

They are telling tales called "Spider Stories."

When African storytellers talk about Kwaku Ananse ("spider man"), they are telling tales called "Spider Stories."

1. (until) In these stories, small, defenseless men or animals are in trouble. They outsmart their larger and more powerful enemies.

_____

_____

2. (before) Many Africans came across the Atlantic Ocean to the Americas in slave ships.

They told these spider stories in their native languages in Africa.

_____

_____

3. (after) They continued to tell these stories.

They arrived in the United States.

_____

_____

4. (as) They told these stories through the years.

They made some changes, such as making the character Ananse into Aunt Nancy in the southern United States.

_____

_____

5. (when) They often repeat the same words to make them stronger.

Storytellers tell these tales to other people.

_____

_____

6. (while) Even today children listen to these tales.

The descendants of the original Africans tell them.

_____

_____

D. _Review of Coordinating and Subordinating Conjunctions_
The following story is a fable from Aesop. Circle the conjunction in parentheses that fits the sentence best. In some cases more than one answer may be correct. Be prepared to explain how the meaning changes in these cases. After you choose the conjunctions, read the three morals that follow and choose the one for this story.

The Milkmaid and Her Pail

A milkmaid carried a large pail of milk on her head (while/or) she was taking it to market. (Because/As) she was walking along the road, she thought of all the money she could get for her milk. She thought to herself: "First, I should buy hens from Farmer Brown, (and/until) they will lay eggs every day. (When/So) I get good eggs from these hens, the parson's wife will buy them from me for a good price. Next, I will buy some new clothes (but/after) I get all this money. (If/Before) I buy these new clothes, I will think carefully about the color. What color will I choose? It will be green (because/but) that color suits me best. Then all the young men will want to speak to me. I will pretend not to see them (if/when) they try to get my attention.

throw (While/Until) I am walking proudly, I'll *toss* my head like this." The pail stayed on her head (because/until) she tossed it. At that moment the pail fell off her head. (Before/After) she could catch it, the milk spilled all over the ground. Finally, she brought her empty pail and sad story home to her mother.

Morals—Which one fits the story of the milkmaid and her pail?

   a. If you teach evil, you must expect more evil.

   b. Do not count your chickens before they are hatched.

   c. It is easy to hate what you know you cannot have.

*E. **Completing Sentences on Your Own** Read the following story about the cowboy hero Pecos Bill. Then complete the sentences that follow with information you learned from this reading. Use the subordinating conjunction given and write a complete clause after the conjunction. Use your own words as much as possible in your answers. Be sure to include correct punctuation. Follow the example.*

Pecos Bill and the Tornado

The great cowboy hero Pecos Bill could successfully ride just about anything, even a wild tornado. One day he was staying in Kansas, and he decided to find the biggest, meanest tornado there. He waited and waited, and then he saw a big tornado in a very dark black and green sky. That tornado also made a loud roar, so that roar woke up farmers from Kansas to China. Soon the tornado came close enough for Pecos Bill to grab it. Bill pushed that wild tornado to the ground and jumped on its back. The tornado tried to throw Bill off, but he held on tight. Then he rode that tornado all the way down to Texas and across the west to California. The storm knocked down forests and mountains all along the way. It also rained enough to fill the Grand Canyon. That tornado continued to try to throw Bill off, but he was just too strong. Finally, Bill fell off because the tornado calmed down to just a small storm. Bill hit the ground so hard that it sank below sea level and became Death Valley. That's the incredible story of how Pecos Bill rode a tornado clear across the west.

1. While _____ _Pecos Bill was staying in Kansas,_ _____ he decided to ride a tornado.

2. He waited and waited before _____

3. The tornado woke up farmers all the way to China when _____

    _____

4. As _____ Bill grabbed it.

5. He held that tornado on the ground until _____

    _____

6. The tornado tried to throw Bill off while _____

    _____

7. After _____ it went all the way to California.

8. That tornado rained and rained until _____

9. When _____ Bill just continued to hold on tight.

10. Bill finally fell off that tornado as _____

11. Bill's fall made Death Valley after _____

F. Finding Sentence Problems   *The stories for these run-on and fragment activities are Aesop's fables. After you complete both of these activities, look back at the morals (page 162) and choose the one that fits each fable.*

1. **Run-ons**   Each sentence below is a run-on.

    a. Find each problem and show how to change it into two simple sentences on the first line.

b. Then write the sentence correctly using the subordinating conjunction in parentheses on the second line. Be sure to use correct punctuation. Follow the example.

The Shepherd and the Wolf

EXAMPLE: A young wolf became alone in the woods his mother decided to leave him there.

A young wolf became alone in the woods. His mother decided to leave him there. (when) A young Wolf became alone in the woods when his mother decided to leave him there.

a. A shepherd found the young wolf he took the animal home to care for him.

_____

(after) _____

b. The wolf was living there the shepherd decided he wanted more lambs.

_____

(while) _____

c. They went out to the fields the shepherd taught the wolf to steal lambs from his neighbors.

_____

(when) _____

d. The wolf was a very good pupil he stole a lamb from the shepherd's own flock.

_____

(until) _____

e. The shepherd realized this he became upset with the wolf.

_____

(as) _____

f. The shepherd tried to show his anger the wolf said, "Was it not you who taught me to steal?"

_____

(before) _____

2. *Fragments*   Find eight fragments in the fable below. Show how to correct each one.

The Fox and the Grapes

As a hungry fox went into a vineyard one day. He saw bunches of sun-ripened grapes on the vines. When he saw the plump and juicy grapes. He could hardly wait to eat them. His mouth watered. As he looked at them on the vines high above him. However, he could not eat them. Until he could reach them. Before he could eat anything. He had to jump up to get them. He could not reach them. After he jumped many times. He continued to jump. Until he finally gave up. While he was walking away from them. He looked up at them and said, "I didn't really want those grapes because they are sour."

3. *Comma splices*   Each sentence below is a comma splice.

a. Find each problem and show how to change it into two simple sentences on the first line.

b. Then write the sentence correctly using the subordinating conjunction in parentheses on the second line. Be sure to use correct punctuation. Follow the example.

Paul Bunyan and Babe Create Minnesota's 10,000 Lakes

EXAMPLE: Minnesota's 10,000 lakes did not exist, Paul Bunyan and Babe lived there.

Minnesota's 10,000 lakes did not exist. Paul Bunyan and Babe lived there. (before) Minnesota's 10,000 lakes did not exist before Paul Bunyan and Babe lived there.

a. One day Babe was not behaving, Paul tied the big blue ox up.

_____

(when)

b. Paul was doing some logging, Babe tried to get free.

_____

(while)

c. Babe got out of the chains, Paul was returning.

_____

(as) _____

d. Babe became free, Paul chased him all over Minnesota.

_____

(after) _____

e. They kept running around, they left their footprints everywhere.

_____

(until) _____

f. It started to rain heavily, all the footprints filled with water.

_____

(after) _____

g. It stopped raining, each footprint turned into a lake.

_____

(before) _____

Discussion/Writing

Your teacher will tell you to answer these questions in writing or through discussion.

1. Which of the stories in this part of this unit have you heard before? Which of them did you enjoy the most? Explain your answer.

2. Do you know any similar stories to the ones in this part of the unit? How are they the same or different in your culture?

PART 4   WRITING PARAGRAPHS—NARRATION/ STORYTELLING/CHRONOLOGY

Read the following creation story and then answer the questions that follow.

How the World *Burst* from an Egg

explode/break from

The Chinese have an ancient story about the creation of the world. First, before the Earth existed, there was nothing at all except a large egg. This egg existed for thousands of years until it broke into two pieces. When this happened, a giant named Phan Ku came out. As one half of the egg fell down and became yin (earth), the other half floated up to become yang (sky). At the same time, the giant pushed the sky up with his hands while he stepped down on the earth. Next, Phan Ku began to grow. As he grew, the space between the sky and earth became bigger. After Phan Ku continued to grow ten feet per day for 18,000 years, he took a rest from holding up the sky. Then he shaped the world by making valleys with his hands and rivers with his fingers. At that time he was old, and he began to cry. His tears rolled down his face until they filled the rivers and streams with water. Finally, he went to sleep forever. As he died, his body changed into different things. His left eye became the sun, and his right eye became the moon. His bones became rocks, and his hair became trees and plants. This is how the world began in a Chinese traditional story.

Paragraph Discussion

1. Does this paragraph follow correct paragraph format? Does it have all of the following?

   ___ a title centered above the paragraph

   ___ correct capitalization of the title

   ___ indenting of the first sentence

   ___ each sentence following the one before

   ___ correct left and right margins

   ___ a capital letter at the beginning of each new sentence

   ___ end punctuation for each sentence

2. Which sentence in this paragraph is the topic sentence? What is the topic and what is the controlling idea?

3. How many supporting sentences are in this paragraph?

4. What kind of information do the supporting sentences give?

5. Does this paragraph have a concluding sentence?

Writing Focus

Paragraph
Organization:
Narration/
Storytelling/
Chronology

Paragraph Organization—Narration and Chronology

Narration

Narration is telling a story or describing an event. The story about how the world came from an egg is a narrative. The paragraphs in the activities of Part 3 of this unit are also narratives. Some of them are myths, some are fables, and some are folktales, but they all tell a traditional story.

Look back at the following pages. Write the story each paragraph tells on the lines next to the story name. Follow the example.

PARAGRAPH	STORY
1. The Beginning of Earth and People (p.155)	the creation of the Earth and the first people
2. Pandora's Box (p.159)	_____
3. A Thousand and One Nights (p.160)	_____
4. The Milkmaid and Her Pail (p.162)	_____
5. Pecos Bill and the Tornado (p.163)	_____
6. The Fox and the Grapes (p.165)	_____

Chronology Review

In Unit Four you learned about using words of chronology such as *first, second, next, then, later,* and *finally* when you write instructions and procedures. You will also find these words in narratives because stories often have a time order to follow. It is usually important to tell the story from the beginning to end using the correct time order. In addition, narratives will also usually include some of the subordinating conjunctions of time such as *before, after, when, while, as,* and *until.*

Look back at the story How the World Burst from an Egg (page 167) and circle all the words of chronology you can find. Then put a line under all the subordinating conjunctions of time.

Practice: Paragraph Organization—Narration and Chronology

A. Words of Chronology   Look back at the story the Milkmaid and Her Pail (page 162). Circle all the words of chronology in that paragraph. Then put a line under each subordinating conjunction of time.

B. Paragraph Analysis *Read the following Native American story about the creation of the Earth. Then do the activity that follows the story.*

The Woman Who Fell from the Sky

According to the Seneca tribe, the Earth began when a woman fell from the sky. At first, there was no Earth. There was only the Great Blue above and water below it. Some people lived in the Great Blue, and one of them was a woman who had strange dreams. After this woman told some men about these dreams, they became afraid of her. Then they pushed her through a hole in the sky, and she fell toward the water below. While she was falling, a bird saw her. This bird made a pillow with his feathers for her to sit on. The bird helped her this way until he called to the other animals in the water to help him. They all wanted to have firm ground for the woman to rest on before the bird put her down. Next, some animals went down into the water in order to bring up mud from the bottom of the sea. After a few of them came up with some mud, they put it on a turtle's back. This was the start of the earth. While some animals continued to bring mud up, others, such as the beaver, were building the mud on the turtle's back into a bigger world. The woman also helped build the earth as she was safely sitting on the turtle's back. Together they all built countries and continents. Finally, they made a whole big round earth. Thus, animals created the earth from mud to help a falling woman, and a turtle continues to hold up the earth today.

1. Fill in the chart on p. 170 with the title and then the topic sentence on the line given. Write the topic sentence on the roof line of the chart exactly as it appears in the paragraph.

2. Fill in the details in the boxes under the topic sentence. Do not write whole sentences from the paragraph. Just write some words. Make sure your notes follow the same chronological order as the story. The boxes are numbered to help you do this. Include words of chronology from the paragraph in your notes. Follow the example in the first box.

3. Write the concluding sentence on the line given for the floor of the house. Write the whole sentence exactly as it appears in the original paragraph.

TITLE: _____

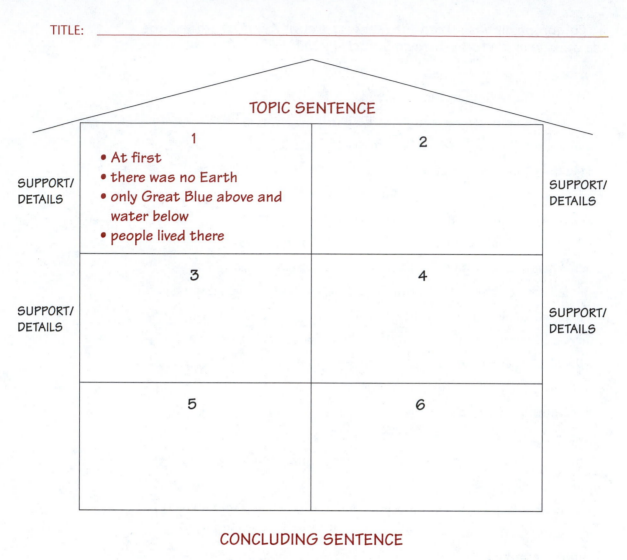

TOPIC SENTENCE

1
- At first
- there was no Earth
- only Great Blue above and water below
- people lived there

SUPPORT/DETAILS

2

SUPPORT/DETAILS

3

SUPPORT/DETAILS

4

SUPPORT/DETAILS

5

6

CONCLUDING SENTENCE

_____
_____
_____

C. Chronology Exercise

1.   Below you will find sentences from the story you read in Part 3 about Pecos Bill. However, these sentences are not in correct chronological order. Write numbers in the spaces next to the sentences to show the correct order according to the story. Work with your partner or group to do this and try not to look back at the story. When you finish the activity, you can check your work by looking back at the paragraph (page 163).

____ a. He saw a very dark sky and heard the roar of a tornado.

____ b. Bill stayed on the tornado all the way to California.

____ c. Bill fell off the tornado because it became a small storm.

____ d. Pecos Bill was staying in Kansas, and he decided to find the biggest tornado there.

____ e. The tornado tried to push him off, but he held on tight.

____ f. The tornado came close enough for Bill to grab it.

____ g. The tornado knocked down trees and mountains along the way.

____ h. Bill created Death Valley from hitting the ground so hard.

____ i. The tornado rained so much it filled the Grand Canyon.

____ j. Bill rode that tornado to Texas.

____ k. Bill pushed the tornado to the ground and jumped on its back.

2. Rewrite the story of Pecos Bill and the Tornado using words of chronology and subordinating conjunctions of time. You may use some of the sentences you wrote for the exercise about the paragraph on pages 163–164. Share your answers with your partner or group and write the new paragraph together. Then share your paragraph with the whole class.

Discussion/Writing

Your teacher will tell you to answer these questions in writing or through discussion.

1. What short myth, legend, fable, or folk story do you know and enjoy from either your own culture or the culture you are now living in? Why do you enjoy this story?

2. Have you ever tried to write your own story or fable? Think of a topic that you might like to write about. How could you create your own story?

Writing Assignment

Picking the Topic

You are going to write a short traditional story that you know well in just one paragraph. This story can be from your own culture or the culture you are now living in. However, be sure to tell this story in your own words. Be sure to include a topic sentence to introduce this story, chronology in your support, and a concluding sentence. If your story is a fable, the concluding sentence can be the moral.

You will choose one of the following to write about.

1. A short myth that explains the creation of something.

2. A short fable with a moral.

3. A short folk story.

Following the Steps in the Writing Process

Before You Write

■ *Step One: Thinking about the Topic/Getting Ideas*
First, think about the writing assignments. What kind of story do you want to tell? Write notes about the story in chronological order. You do not need to write complete sentences and don't worry about organization for this part.

A Myth

A Fable

A Folk Story

Now choose one of these topics to write your paragraph about.

■ *Step Two: Organizing Your Thoughts and Ideas*
Think about a topic sentence. Imagine that your reader does not know this story, so your first sentence must introduce it.

Topic Sentence

a. What kind of story will you write?

_____

b. What is the main idea of this story? What is your topic and what is your controlling idea?

_____

c. Write your topic sentence on the chart at the end of this unit (page 176).

Support

d. Look back at your notes for Step One on page 172 and circle the details you want to include. Make sure your paragraph has enough details. Make sure the details are important to your story. Also be sure to tell the story chronologically and to include words to show this order.

e. Write your ideas for support on the chart at the end of this unit (page 176). You do not need to write complete sentences on this chart, but you should include specific words from the chart in Step One on page 172.

Concluding Sentence

f. Write a concluding sentence. If your story is a fable, write the moral as the concluding sentence. For other kinds of stories, you may restate the topic sentence or give a short summary in your concluding sentence. Write this sentence on the chart on page 176.

g. Write a title for this paragraph on the chart at the end of this unit (page 176).

■ *Step Three: Getting Feedback about the Chart*
Show your chart to another person. Your teacher may ask you to work with a partner and complete a review of your chart/outline. Use the review sheet on page 204 in the Appendix for this feedback.

When You Write

■ *Step Four: Writing the First Draft (Rough Draft)*
Write your first draft of the paragraph. Do not worry about perfect grammar, spelling, punctuation, or capitalization for this draft. Make sure you write this first draft using the ideas on the chart/outline (page 176).

Be sure to include the following in your rough draft:

- Make a title.
- Begin the paragraph with a topic sentence.
- Support your topic sentence with details about the story. Use the information for support/details on your chart in your paragraph. Make sure you have enough support.
- Use both coordinating conjunctions and subordinating conjunctions in your sentences.
- Use at least three subordinating conjunctions of time.
- Use at least three words or expressions of time to show chronology.
- Try to use at least three vocabulary words from this unit.
- End your paragraph with a concluding sentence.

After You Write

Check Your Work
After you finish writing the first draft, read your paragraph again. Check your work for the following. Do this before you show it to anyone else.

☐ This paragraph tells one of the following kinds of stories:
  - a myth
  - a fable
  - a folk story

☐ This paragraph has a title.

☐ This paragraph has a topic sentence.

☐ The paragraph is a narrative.

☐ This paragraph has enough sentences of support/details to tell the story.

☐ All of the details/support relate to the story

☐ The support/details are in chronological order.

☐ I tried to use at least three words or expressions of time to show chronological order.

☐ This paragraph has a concluding sentence.

☐ I tried to use three vocabulary words from this lesson in the paragraph.

☐ I wrote some simple sentences and some sentences with conjunctions.

☐ I used three different subordinating conjunctions of time in my sentences.

☐ I checked each sentence for fragments.

☐ I checked each sentence for run-ons and comma splices.

This paragraph has correct paragraph form as follows:

- ☐ The title is centered above the paragraph.
- ☐ The title has correct capitalization.
- ☐ The title does not end in a period.
- ☐ I indented the first sentence of the paragraph.
- ☐ I have correct margins on the left and right.
- ☐ I did not put punctuation (period, comma, question mark) at the beginning of a new line.
- ☐ I double-spaced (skipped a space after every line).
- ☐ All of my sentences follow one another. (I did not go to the next line with a new sentence.)

■ *Step Five: Getting Feedback about the First Draft*
Show someone your first draft of the paragraph. Your teacher will decide the type of feedback you will receive for the first draft. It may be with a partner or from the teacher or both ways. For review with a partner, use the sheets on pages 205–206 in the Appendix.

■ *Step Six: Making Changes*
After you receive feedback, make some changes. First, decide if you want to change your topic sentence. Then decide if you want to change your supporting sentences by adding new ones or taking out some. Decide if you want to change your concluding sentence. After you make these changes, look at all the grammar, punctuation, spelling, and capitalization. Make any necessary changes in these things as well.

■ *Step Seven: The Final Draft*
Type your final draft on a computer. Try to make this paragraph as perfect as you can.

Organizing Your Thoughts for Writing

TITLE: _____

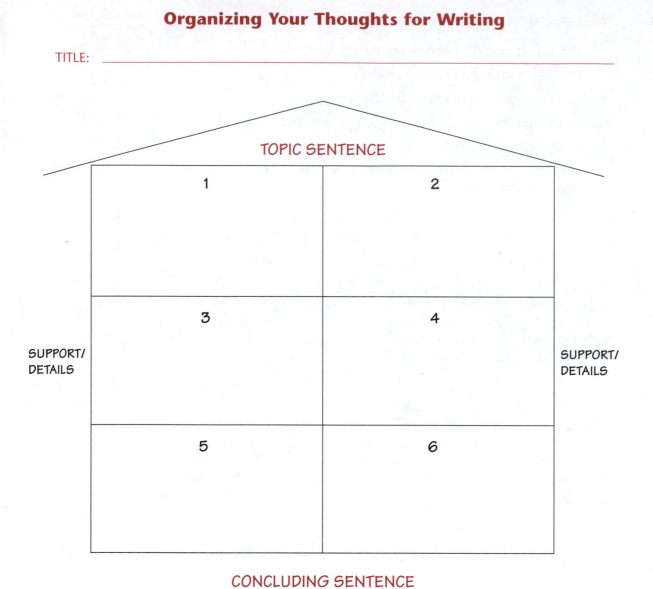

TOPIC SENTENCE

1	2
3	4
5	6

SUPPORT/DETAILS

SUPPORT/DETAILS

CONCLUDING SENTENCE

_____
_____
_____

Appendix

From Paragraphs to Essays (pages 178–187)

Journal Writing (page 188)

Timed Writing (page 189)

Feedback: Peer Review (pages 190–206)

Sentence Pattern Chart (page 207)

Sentence Combining Chart (page 208)

Vocabulary Index (page 209)

Skills Index (pages 211)

FROM PARAGRAPHS TO ESSAYS

In this book you are learning about and practicing paragraph writing with different kinds of organization. Sometimes in your college classes, you may have to write paragraphs for specific assignments or as answers on tests. However, much of college writing involves longer pieces of work called *essays* (sometimes called *compositions*). Paragraphs and essays have some similarities and some differences as discussed below.

Review of Paragraphs

Read the following paragraph from Unit One and answer the questions that follow.

Getting Support in Your Classes

Students can work with their instructors and classmates to increase their chances of succeeding in school. For one thing, they should understand that instructors are available for questions and extra help. For example, students can visit instructors during office hours or make an appointment to see their instructors at other times. In addition, finding a "buddy" in the class is another kind of support. You may want to work with this person on homework and other assignments, or you can contact him/her just to ask questions. Also, students can form a study group with other students in the class. Often students in these groups work together outside their class. At these study sessions they review their notes, exchange opinions about materials and assignments from the class, and help each other with questions or in weak areas of understanding. Students should try to take advantage of some of these ways to help themselves in their classes.

Questions

1. Does this paragraph have three parts as follows?
   - a topic sentence—If your answer is yes, underline this sentence.
   - support related to the topic sentence
   - a concluding sentence—If your answer is yes, underline this sentence.

2. What kind of support does this paragraph contain? How many details are in this paragraph? Does each detail have more support?

Expanding Paragraphs into Essays

Read the essay below about the same topic as the paragraph above. Then answer the questions that follow the essay.

Getting Support in Your Classes

Choosing to attend college is an important decision, and college classes usually require much hard work. Students often have many different assignments and requirements to complete for each of their classes. In addition, many students may be busy with a job and/or family responsibilities while they are going to school. In any case, students need to find the best way to complete their classes successfully in order to reach the final goals of their education. One way is for students to work with both their instructors and classmates to increase their chances of success in school.

For one thing, students should understand that instructors are available for questions and extra help. For example, students can visit instructors during office hours or make an appointment to see their instructors at other times. In this way, students can receive personal attention and can ask specific questions about the work in the class. Also, some students may want to email their instructors. If the email exchange does not answer all the student's questions, then s/he may want to visit the instructor during office hours or make an appointment to speak to the instructor personally.

In addition, finding a "buddy" in the class is another kind of support. In establishing a "buddy," it is often helpful to exchange phone numbers or email addresses during the first week or two of classes. Then these students may contact each other with questions about the class, such as how to complete homework or other assignments, due dates, etc. Having a buddy can be especially helpful when a student is absent from a class and needs to find out about the missed work and assignments.

Students can also form a study group with other students in the class. Most often students in these groups work together outside their class. At these study sessions they review their notes, exchange opinions about materials and assignments from the class, and help each other with questions or weak areas of understanding. Studying for exams together can be very helpful because students in the group may have different strengths and weaknesses. Therefore, they can share different ways of understanding the material in order to help each other prepare for tests.

Attending college and keeping up with the work can be very demanding. Communicating with instructors, having a buddy in the class, and participating in study groups are all ways to help a student succeed. Thus, students should try to take advantage of some of these ways to help themselves in their classes.

Questions

1. How many paragraphs are in this essay?

2. What is the purpose of the first paragraph?

3. What is the purpose of the next three paragraphs?

4. Are any of the details in this essay the same as the details in the paragraph on page 21?

5. What is the purpose of the last paragraph in this essay?

Paragraph to Essay Discussion

General Organization

A. A paragraph is a group of sentences about one topic. A paragraph usually has three parts:

- a topic sentence

- support/details

- a concluding sentence

B. An essay is a group of paragraphs about one topic. An essay also has three parts as follows:

- an introduction (one paragraph)

- support—at least one paragraph with details

- a conclusion (one paragraph)

Circle the introduction of the sample essay on pages 177–178. Draw a box around the conclusion of that essay.

Introductions/Main Ideas

A. The first sentence of a paragraph contains the main idea. It is called a *topic sentence*. All the details and support in the paragraph should be about the same topic of this sentence.

B. The first paragraph of an essay is called the *introduction*, and it contains several sentences. It provides general information so that the reader will know a little about the topic of the essay. A good introduction will make the reader interested in the subject and want to read more about it.

How many sentences are in the introduction of the sample essay above? What general information do you learn in this introduction?

C. The last sentence of the introduction of an essay tells the reader the main idea or the specific topic of the essay. It is called a *thesis statement*. All of the paragraphs of the essay should relate to this thesis statement.

Find the thesis statement in the essay above and underline it. What does this sentence tell the reader about the main idea of this essay? (What information should the reader expect to find in the essay after reading this thesis statement?)

Paragraph Information/Details and Support

A. A *paragraph* should have several sentences of support or details related to the topic sentence. For each new detail, it is a good idea to have more information to explain this support.

B. An *essay* should have at least one (but usually more than one) paragraph of details/support after the introduction. These paragraphs are called the *body* of the essay.

How many body paragraphs are in the sample essay above? Number each of these paragraphs in the margin space to the left.

C. Each *body paragraph* should have a topic sentence and support. The details in this support should all relate to the topic sentence. In addition, this topic sentence relates to the thesis statement. In other words, each topic sentence should explain one part of the main idea in the thesis statement.

Underline the topic sentence of each body paragraph in the sample essay above. Is each of these sentences about the main idea in the thesis statement?

How many sentences of support are in each body paragraph of the sample essay? Do all of the details in each body paragraph support the topic sentence of that paragraph?

D. In an essay a body paragraph may or may not have a concluding sentence.

Can you find a concluding sentence in the body paragraphs of the sample essay?

Conclusions

A. The concluding sentence of a paragraph is more general than the details/support. It reviews the main idea or summarizes the information in the paragraph.

B. The conclusion of an essay should be general. It may review the main idea or summarize the essay. The concluding paragraph should have more than one sentence.

How many sentences does the concluding paragraph of the sample essay contain? Does this conclusion review the main idea or summarize the essay?

Look at the following diagrams of the organization of a paragraph and an essay. Does the sample paragraph above follow this diagram? Does the sample essay above follow this diagram? Be prepared to explain your answer.

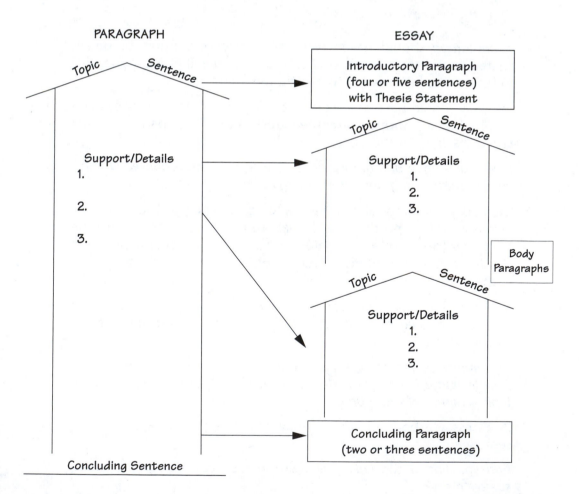

What similarities do you see between the paragraph and the essay?

1. They both have three main parts. *Number these three parts on the diagrams above.*

2. They both begin with more general information, give more specific information in the second part, and end with more general information.

   paragraph: topic sentence = general/main idea

   details/support = more specific information

   concluding sentence = general

   essay: introductory paragraph and thesis statement = general/ main idea

   details/support in paragraphs = more specific information

   concluding paragraph = general

3. They both have a sentence with the main idea:

   - topic sentence (paragraph)

   - thesis statement (essay)

4. They both give support in the second part, such as examples, facts, reasons, etc. In a paragraph there are several sentences for this support. In an essay, there are paragraphs with this support.

How are the paragraph and essay different?

1. A paragraph is shorter than an essay. The topic of an essay is usually more general, so the essay is longer.

2. A paragraph has one indentation at the beginning. All sentences follow one another in a paragraph. An essay has several indentations, one for the beginning of each new paragraph.

Practice: Expanding Paragraphs into Essays

A. Look back at the sample essay on pages 179–180 and fill in the chart on the next page with information from this essay.

   - Write the thesis statement exactly as you see it in the essay on the lines in the box for the introduction.

   - Write the topic sentence for each paragraph on the lines for the roof of the house.

   - Write some words, not sentences for the details/support for each paragraph. Follow the example on page 184.

   - Write some words, not sentences from the conclusion on the lines in the box.

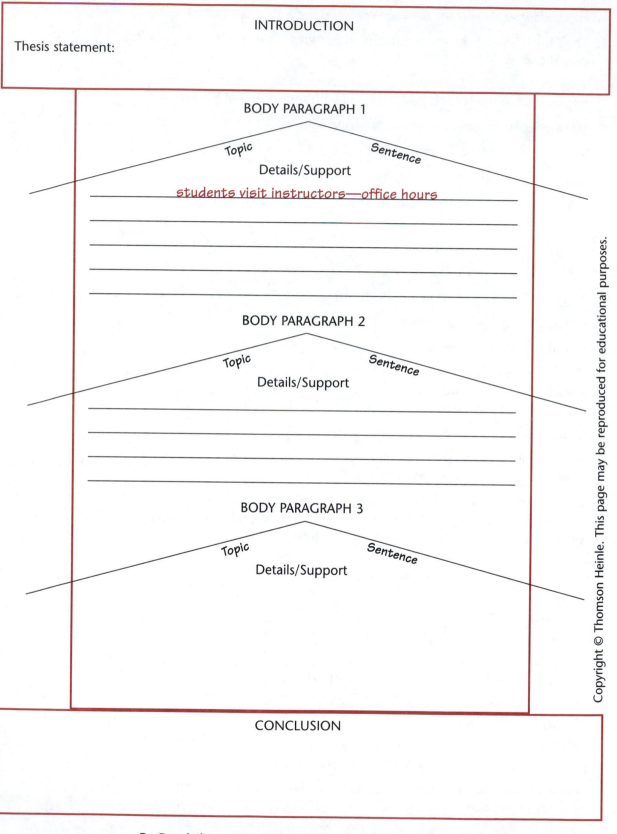

INTRODUCTION

Thesis statement:

BODY PARAGRAPH 1

Topic   Sentence

Details/Support

students visit instructors—office hours

BODY PARAGRAPH 2

Topic   Sentence

Details/Support

BODY PARAGRAPH 3

Topic   Sentence

Details/Support

CONCLUSION

B. Read the paragraph about job interviews in Unit Four on page 106. Then read the following essay about the same subject. Fill in the chart below the essay with information from this essay.

Job Interviews

Looking for a job can be a difficult and stressful experience. A job search usually includes several steps, such as identifying a job to apply for, filling out an application, and going to an interview. When a person reaches the interview step, there is a good chance s/he might get the job. An interview is the applicant's chance to sell himself/herself to the employer, and the following procedure can make the experience a successful one.

First, you should get ready for the interview by taking stock of yourself. In other words, you should think about your strongest abilities and qualities. Consider many different areas of your life, such as your education, experience with this kind of work, and your personality. Think about how you want to present this information to your possible future employer so that s/he sees you as the best person for the job. This will help you on the interview and later at the workplace.

Second, preparing for the questions and answers is very important. For instance, you can research both the company and the specific job. You should look on the Internet or find people to discuss the company and the duties of this job with. Also, you could practice answering possible interview questions. This might include preparing a short review of your strengths, background, and goals. Often interviewers ask about your weaknesses as well as your strengths, so you may want to think of the best way to present that information.

Next, it is important to make a good impression during the interview, so you should make sure you present yourself well in person. For one thing, you should dress appropriately for the type of business and job. In addition, you should arrive a little early for your appointment. During the interview it is important to present your information and interest in the job with a positive attitude. You should also make sure you answer each question completely.

Finally, after the interview it is a good idea to send a thank-you note. This will help the interviewer remember you and can make you "different" from the other candidates for the job. The note should be short and should not include new information about yourself. The purpose of this note is not to continue the interview but to remind the employer about you and your abilities.

An interview can be the most important part of getting a job, so it is important to prepare yourself well for this experience. It can be stressful to go through this process, but it can also be rewarding. Therefore, following this procedure of preparation, good interview practices, and follow-up can help you get the job.

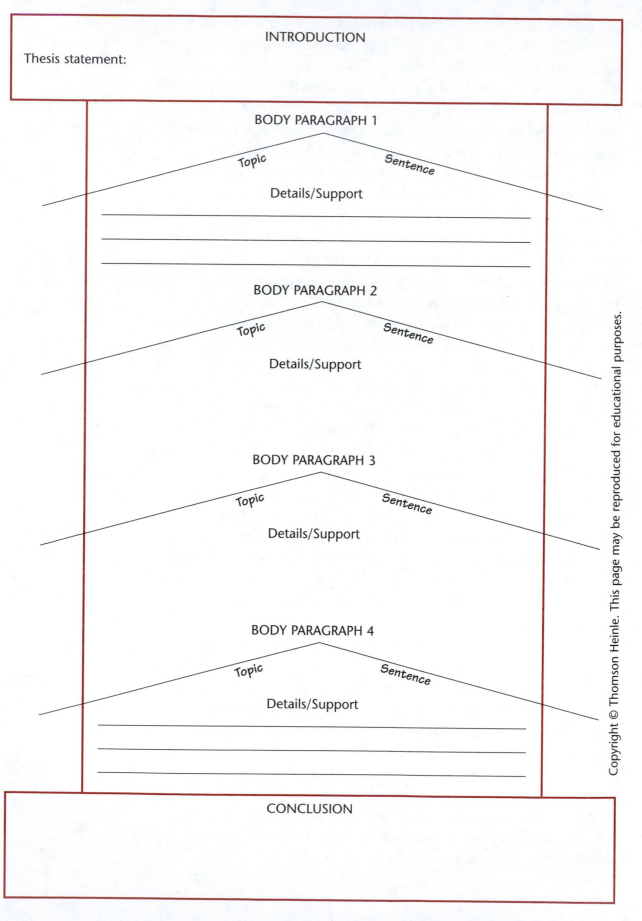

INTRODUCTION

Thesis statement:

BODY PARAGRAPH 1

Topic   Sentence

Details/Support

BODY PARAGRAPH 2

Topic   Sentence

Details/Support

BODY PARAGRAPH 3

Topic   Sentence

Details/Support

BODY PARAGRAPH 4

Topic   Sentence

Details/Support

CONCLUSION

C. Choose one of the following paragraphs to expand into an essay. Make a chart like the ones above and write the thesis statement, topic sentences, notes for each body paragraph, and notes for a conclusion.

Your teacher may also ask you to write the entire essay after you organize it on the chart.

Choices:

Unit One: Preparing for Classes—page 14
              Support Across the Campus—pages 23–24
Unit Four: Job Applications—page 98
Unit Five: Technology in the Classroom—page 127
              Distance Learning: An Excellent Educational Experience—
                   page 139
              No Laptops in the Classroom—page 142

JOURNAL WRITING

Journal writing is often a personal kind of writing. It usually does not have a grade or corrections. Instead, journal writing gives students a chance to communicate ideas without thinking about organization, grammar, and details, such as spelling and punctuation. Students often feel more comfortable writing in a journal than writing assignments for a grade.

Your teacher may want you to do some journal writing as you go through this book. When you write in your journal, feel free to include your thoughts and opinions about the topics your teacher assigns. In addition, sometimes your journal writing can help you with ideas for the more formal academic writing you will complete for a grade.

When you see the icon: ✏️➤ in this book, it indicates a good topic or writing assignment for a journal entry.

TIMED WRITING

The writing you are learning about and practicing in this book follows the process of writing (or *process writing*). This kind of writing takes place over a period of time, perhaps a week or two. However, sometimes you will need to write in a more limited amount of time. This kind of writing is called *timed writing.* In timed writing the writer has a specific amount of time to think about, plan, organize, write, and check his or her work. Sometimes the writer may see the question or topic to write about before the time of writing. Sometimes the writer may see the topic or question for the first time at the time of writing. For some people this type of writing can be very difficult and stressful. Timed writing is common in college level classes. As a college student your teachers may require you to complete timed writing assignments in many different kinds of courses, including your English/ESL classes. For example, teachers may ask students to write answers in paragraph form during in-class exams.

   You might not have much time in this kind of assignment, but you can still follow some of the steps in the process as follows:

Step 1   **Understand the Question.**   Make sure you understand the question! If you do not understand it, ask the instructor about it. You cannot answer the question properly if you do not understand it.

Step 2   **Brainstorm and Plan.**   Before you write, you should make a basic plan of your ideas. You can spend the first 5 to 10 minutes thinking about your ideas and organizing them. The amount of time will depend on how much time you have to complete the assignment. If you make a general plan of your ideas, it will be easier to write in the time you are given. If the instructor allows it, you can brainstorm a list or make an outline or chart of your ideas on a piece of paper. Do not worry about writing full sentences. Writing words and notes should be enough. This step should help you to decide which ideas you will write about and to organize them. You should try to do this quickly. Be careful not to write too much or spend too much time on this step.

Step 3   **Write.**   The actual writing will take most of your time. Use the notes you made in the first few minutes of planning and try to write quickly. Try to write correctly, but think about how you are answering the question. Also, think about the organization of your ideas as you write.

Step 4   **Revise and Edit.**   You may not have too much time for revising or editing, but you should try to leave the last 5 to 10 minutes for checking your work. Look for fragments, comma splices, and run-ons, and check the grammar, spelling, and punctuation as best you can.

FEEDBACK: PEER REVIEW

Getting feedback about your planning and writing can help you during the writing process. You probably usually receive suggestions and corrections from your teacher, but other people can often provide helpful feedback as well. For example, other students in your class (your peers) might be able to help you with your ideas and organization and even sometimes with grammar and sentence structure.

Your teacher may ask you to participate in peer review from time to time, using the sheets provided on the following pages. When you participate in these peer reviews, you will answer the specific questions on the sheets, which apply to the writing assignments in each unit of this book. Your teacher will decide how many of these peer review sheets you will complete for each writing assignment. Try to be honest when you answer questions about your classmates' work. Be sure to discuss both the good points and any parts you think should be changed.

Important: Some students question whether other students can provide helpful feedback because they are learners themselves. Of course, your peers will not be able to give you as much feedback as your teacher can. However, it is always good to hear what other people think of your work and to see what other people write about a particular topic (when you review their papers).

Your peers may not be able to help you with everything or tell you all of your mistakes. However, they can probably help you think about how you answered the topic question, or they may be able to help you organize your thoughts. They might also be able to help you with some specific areas that you have studied together in this class, such as sentence writing.

UNIT ONE PEER REVIEW SHEET
Example Paragraph Chart

Your Name: _____   Partner's Name: _____

1. Exchange charts with a partner. Read your partner's chart and answer
    the following questions:

    - Does your partner's chart have a topic sentence about new student
      information, making a class schedule, or study habits?

                    yes   no

    - Is the topic sentence general enough for all the information in the
      paragraph?

                    yes   no

    - Does your partner's chart have enough examples about informa-
      tion for a new student, making a class schedule, or study habits?

                    yes   no

    - Do all of the examples on the chart relate to the topic sentence?

                    yes   no

    - Does your partner's chart have support (more information) for each
      example?

                    yes   no

2. Do you have any questions for your partner about this paragraph? Are
    there any parts of the chart you do not understand?

    _____

    _____

    _____

    _____

    _____

    _____

    _____

    _____

    _____

    _____

    _____

UNIT ONE PEER REVIEW SHEET
First Draft of Paragraph

Your Name: _____   Partner's Name: _____

1. Exchange papers with a partner. Read your partner's paper and check the paragraph using the following checklist.

    This paragraph discusses one of the following:
    - important information for new students
    - making a class schedule
    - study habits to improve (or successful study habits)

    This paragraph has a title.

    This paragraph has a topic sentence.

    This paragraph has three or four examples.

    All of the examples are about the topic sentence.

    The writer added more information about each example.

    The writer used three transitions at the beginning of sentences.

    The writer used three vocabulary words from this unit in the paragraph.

    The paragraph has no fragments (missing subjects or verbs).

    This paragraph has correct paragraph form as follows:

    The title is centered above the paragraph.

    The title has correct capitalization.

    The title does not end in a period.

    The writer indented the first sentence of the paragraph.

    The writer used correct margins on the left and right.

    The writer did not put punctuation (period, comma, question mark) at the beginning of a new line.

    The writer double-spaced (skipped a space after every line).

    All of the sentences follow one another. (The writer did not go to the next line with a new sentence.)

2. Tell your partner what you liked about his/her paragraph. (Use the space below to write some notes about this.)

    _____

    _____

3. Do you have any questions about this paragraph? Is there anything you might change in this paragraph?

    <u>Do not</u> write any changes on your partner's paper. Just discuss your suggestions. Think about the items on the checklist above when you make your suggestions. Your partner will do the same for you. (Use the space below to write some notes about this.)

    _____

    _____

UNIT TWO PEER REVIEW SHEET
Descriptive Paragraph Chart

Your Name: _____   Partner's Name: _____

1. Exchange charts with a partner. Read your partner's chart and answer the following questions:

   - Does your partner's chart have a topic sentence about a kind of body art or about a celebration or ritual that includes some kind of body art?

     yes   no

   If you said yes, what is the specific kind of body art or celebration with body art?

   _____

   _____

   - Does the chart have enough details/support? Is it a vivid description?

     yes   no

   - Does all of the support describe the body art or celebration and body art?

     yes   no

2. Do you have any questions for your partner about this essay? Are there any parts of the chart you do not understand?

   _____
   _____
   _____
   _____
   _____
   _____
   _____
   _____
   _____
   _____
   _____

UNIT TWO PEER REVIEW SHEET
First Draft of Paragraph

Your Name: Partner's Name:

1. Exchange papers with a classmate. Read his/her paper and check the paragraph using the following checklist.

   This paragraph discusses one of the following:
   - your partner's (or friend's or relative's) body art/decoration
   - body art or decoration in your partner's culture
   - a specific ceremony or celebration that includes body art/decoration

   This paragraph has a title.

   This paragraph has a topic sentence.

   This paragraph has at least five or six sentences of description.

   All of the descriptive sentences relate to the topic sentence.

   The writer used three vocabulary words from this lesson in the paragraph.

   The writer used several sentence patterns, such as subject + verb, subject + verb + object, and linking verbs with adjectives, nouns, and prepositions.

   The paragraph has no fragments (missing subjects or verbs).

   This paragraph has correct paragraph form as follows:

   The title is centered above the paragraph.

   The title has correct capitalization.

   The title does not end in a period.

   The writer indented the first sentence of the paragraph.

   The writer used correct margins on the left and right.

   The writer did not put punctuation (period, comma, question mark) at the beginning of a new line.

   The writer double-spaced (skipped a space after every line).

   All of the sentences follow one another. (The writer did not go to the next line with a new sentence.)

2. Tell your partner what you liked about his/her paragraph or what s/he did well in this paragraph. (Use the space below to write some notes about this.)

   _____

   _____

3. Do you have any questions about this paragraph? Is there anything you might change in this paragraph?

   <u>Do not</u> write any changes on your partner's paper. Just discuss your suggestions. Think about the items on the checklist above when you make your suggestions. Your partner will do the same for you. (Use the space below to write some notes about this.)

   _____

   _____

UNIT THREE PEER REVIEW SHEET
Paragraph with Facts Chart

Your Name: _____   Partner's Name: _____

1. Exchange charts with a partner. Read your partner's chart and answer the following questions:

   • Does your partner's chart have a topic sentence about family history or about a biography?

                   yes   no

   • Is the topic sentence general enough for all the information in the paragraph?

                   yes   no

   • Does the chart have enough details/support? Are there enough facts in the paragraph?

                   yes   no

   • Does all of the support relate to the family history or biography of a specific person?

                   yes   no

   • Does your partner's chart have a concluding sentence?

                   yes   no

2. Do you have any questions for your partner about this essay? Are there any parts of the chart you do not understand?

   _____

   _____

   _____

   _____

   _____

   _____

   _____

   _____

   _____

   _____

   _____

   _____

UNIT THREE PEER REVIEW SHEET
First Draft of Paragraph

Your Name: Partner's Name:

1. Exchange papers with a classmate. Read his/her paper and check the paragraph using the following checklist.

   This paragraph discusses one of the following:
   - the writer's family history
   - a biography/autobiography

   This paragraph has a title.

   This paragraph has a topic sentence.

   This paragraph has at least five to seven sentences of support/details.

   All of the details/support relate to the topic sentence.

   The support/details include facts, such as names, dates, and numbers.

   For a biography or autobiography the writer included accomplishments/achievement of this person.

   This paragraph has a concluding sentence.

   The concluding sentence restates the topic sentence (main idea).

   The writer used three vocabulary words from this lesson in the paragraph.

   The writer wrote some simple sentences and some sentences with coordinating conjunctions.

   The writer used three different coordinating conjunctions in the sentences.

   The paragraph has no fragments (missing subjects or verbs).

   The paragraph has no run-ons or comma splices.

This paragraph has correct paragraph form as follows:

   The title is centered above the paragraph.

   The title has correct capitalization.

   The title does not end in a period.

   The writer indented the first sentence of the paragraph.

   The paragraph has correct margins on the left and right.

   The writer did not put punctuation (period, comma, question mark) at the beginning of a new line.

   The writer double-spaced (skipped a space after every line).

   All of the sentences follow one another. (The writer did not go to the next line with a new sentence.)

UNIT THREE PEER REVIEW SHEET—CONTINUED
First Draft of Paragraph

2. Tell your partner what you liked about his/her paragraph or what s/he did well in this paragraph. (Use the space below to write some notes about this.)

_____

_____

3. Do you have any questions about this paragraph? Is there anything you might change in this paragraph?

   <u>Do not</u> write any changes on your partner's paper. Just discuss your suggestions. Think about the items on the checklist above when you make your suggestions. Your partner will do the same for you. (Use the space below to write some notes about this.)

   _____

   _____

   _____

   _____

   _____

UNIT FOUR PEER REVIEW SHEET
Instructions/Procedure Paragraph Chart

Your Name: Partner's Name:

1. Exchange charts with a partner. Read your partner's chart and answer the following questions:

   • Does your partner's chart have a topic sentence about instructions for using a machine/equipment or about a procedure?

   yes   no

   • Is the topic sentence general enough for all the information in the paragraph?

   yes   no

   • Does your partner's chart have enough steps about using the machine/equipment or about the procedure?

   yes   no

   • Are all of the steps in chronological order?

   yes   no

   • Does your partner's chart have support (more information) for each step?

   yes   no

   • Does your partner have a concluding sentence?

   yes   no

2. Do you have any questions for your partner about this paragraph? Are there any parts of the chart you do not understand?

   _____

   _____

   _____

   _____

   _____

   _____

   _____

   _____

   _____

   _____

UNIT FOUR PEER REVIEW SHEET
First Draft of Paragraph

Your Name: _____   Partner's Name: _____

1. Exchange papers with a partner. Read your partner's paper and check the paragraph using the following checklist.

____ This paragraph discusses one of the following:
  • instructions for using a machine or a piece of equipment
  • a procedure

____ This paragraph has a title.

____ This paragraph has a topic sentence.

____ This paragraph has at least 4 or 5 steps for the instructions or procedure.

____ All of the steps relate to the topic sentence.

____ The steps are in chronological order.

____ The writer explained some of the steps with more supporting sentences.

____ This paragraph has a concluding sentence.

____ The concluding sentence reviews/summarizes the steps.

____ The writer used three vocabulary words from this lesson in the paragraph.

____ The writer used at least three introductory transitions showing chronological order.

____ The writer used at least three other introductory transitions in this paragraph.

____ The writer wrote some simple sentences and some sentences with coordinating conjunctions.

____ The writer used three different coordinating conjunctions.

____ This paragraph has no fragments (missing subjects or verbs).

____ This paragraph has no run-ons or comma splices.

This paragraph has correct paragraph form as follows:

____ The title is centered above the paragraph.

____ The title has correct capitalization.

____ The title does not end in a period.

____ The writer indented the first sentence of the paragraph.

____ The writer used correct margins on the left and right.

____ The writer did not put punctuation (period, comma, question mark) at the beginning of a new line.

____ The writer double-spaced (skipped a space after every line).

____ All of the sentences follow one another. (The writer did not go to the next line with a new sentence.)

UNIT FOUR PEER REVIEW SHEET—CONTINUED
First Draft of Paragraph

2. Tell your partner what you liked about his/her paragraph. (Use the space below to write some notes about this.)

_____

_____

_____

_____

3. Do you have any questions about this paragraph? Is there anything you might change in this paragraph?

   <u>Do not</u> write any changes on your partner's paper. Just discuss your suggestions. Think about the items on the checklist above when you make your suggestions. Your partner will do the same for you. (Use the space below to write some notes about this.)

_____

_____

_____

_____

_____

_____

_____

_____

UNIT FIVE PEER REVIEW SHEET
Opinion Paragraph Chart

Your Name: _____   Partner's Name: _____

1. Exchange charts with a partner. Read your partner's chart and answer the following questions:

   • Does your partner's chart have a topic sentence about an opinion?

   yes   no

   If you said yes, is the topic sentence an opinion about teachers using technology in the classroom or requiring students to use technology for their assignments? What is the opinion?

   _____

   _____

   _____

   • Does the chart have enough support for the opinion?

   yes   no

   • Does the support give reasons for the writer's opinion?

   yes   no

   • Does the chart have a concluding sentence?

   yes   no

2. Do you have any questions for your partner about this paragraph? Are there any parts of the chart you do not understand?

   _____

   _____

   _____

   _____

   _____

   _____

   _____

   _____

   _____

   _____

   _____

   _____

UNIT FIVE PEER REVIEW SHEET
First Draft of Paragraph

Your Name: _____   Partner's Name: _____

1. Exchange papers with a classmate. Read his/her paper and check the paragraph using the following checklist.

   This paragraph discusses one of the following:
   - why the writer thinks teachers should use technology in the classroom
   - why the writer thinks they should not use technology in the classroom
   - why the writer thinks requiring students to use computers for assignments is a good idea
   - why the writer thinks requiring students to use computers for assignments is not a good idea

   This paragraph has a title.

   This paragraph has a topic sentence.

   This paragraph has at least five to seven sentences of support/details.

   All of the details are reasons and support for those reasons.

   All of the reasons support the topic sentence.

   This paragraph has a concluding sentence.

   The writer used three vocabulary words from this lesson in the paragraph.

   The writer wrote some simple sentences and some sentences with coordinating conjunctions.

   The writer used the subordinating conjunctions *because* and *if* in some sentences.

   This paragraph has no fragments (missing subjects or verbs).

   This paragraph has no run-ons or comma splices.

This paragraph has correct paragraph form as follows:

   The title is centered above the paragraph.

   The title has correct capitalization.

   The title does not end in a period.

   The writer indented the first sentence of the paragraph.

   The writer used correct margins on the left and right.

   The writer did not put punctuation (period, comma, question mark) at the beginning of a new line.

   The writer double-spaced (skipped a space after every line).

   All of the sentences follow one another. (The writer did not go to the next line with a new sentence.)

UNIT FIVE PEER REVIEW SHEET—CONTINUED
First Draft of Paragraph

2. Tell your partner what you liked about his/her paragraph or what s/he did well in this paragraph. (Use the space below to write some notes about this.)

_____

_____

_____

_____

_____

_____

3. Do you have any questions about this essay? Is there anything you might change in this essay?

   <u>Do not</u> write any changes on your partner's paper. Just discuss your suggestions. Think about the items on the checklist above when you make your suggestions. Your partner will do the same for you. (Use the space below to write some notes about this.)

_____

_____

_____

_____

_____

_____

_____

UNIT SIX PEER REVIEW SHEET
Narrative Paragraph Chart

Your Name: _____   Partner's Name: _____

1. Exchange charts with a partner. Read your partner's chart and answer the following questions:

   • Does your partner's chart have a topic sentence to introduce the narrative?

   yes   no

   If you said yes, what is the story about? Is it a myth, a fable, or a folk story?

   _____

   _____

   • Does the chart have enough details/support for the paragraph?

   yes   no

   • Does all of the support fit the story?

   yes   no

   • Are the details in chronological order?

   yes   no

   • Does the chart have a concluding sentence?

   yes   no

2. Do you have any questions for your partner about this paragraph? Are there any parts of the chart you do not understand?

   _____

   _____

   _____

   _____

   _____

   _____

   _____

UNIT SIX PEER REVIEW SHEET
First Draft of Paragraph

Your Name:	Partner's Name:

1. Exchange papers with a classmate. Read his/her paper and check the paragraph using the following checklist.

   This paragraph tells one of the following stories:
   - a myth
   - a fable
   - a folk story

   This paragraph has a title.

   This paragraph has a topic sentence.

   This paragraph has at least 5 to 7 sentences of support/details.

   The paragraph is a narrative.

   All of the details/support relate to the story.

   The support/details are in chronological order.

   The writer used at least three words or expressions of time to show chronological order.

   This paragraph has a concluding sentence.

   The writer used three vocabulary words from this lesson in the paragraph.

   The writer wrote some simple sentences and some sentences with coordinating conjunctions.

   The writer used three different subordinating conjunctions of time.

   This paragraph has no fragments (missing subjects or verbs).

   This paragraph has no run-ons or comma splices.

This paragraph has correct paragraph form as follows:

   The title is centered above the paragraph.

   The title has correct capitalization.

   The title does not end in a period.

   The writer indented the first sentence of the paragraph.

   The writer used correct margins on the left and right.

   The writer did not put punctuation (period, comma, question mark) at the beginning of a new line.

   The writer double-spaced (skipped a space after every line).

   All of the sentences follow one another. (The writer did not go to the next line with a new sentence.)

UNIT SIX PEER REVIEW SHEET—CONTINUED
First Draft of Paragraph

2. Tell your partner what you liked about his/her paragraph or what s/he did well in this paragraph. (Use the space below to write some notes about this.)

_____

_____

_____

_____

_____

_____

_____

3. Do you have any questions about this paragraph? Is there anything you might change in this paragraph?

Do not write any changes on your partner's paper. Just discuss your suggestions. Think about the items on the checklist above when you make your suggestions. Your partner will do the same for you. (Use the space below to write some notes about this.)

_____

_____

_____

_____

Sentence Pattern Chart

Subject + Verb (no object)	Subject + Verb + Object

Subject + Verb
 	
Jane goes to work five days a week.
S   V
John talked for an hour on the telephone.
S   V
Sue listens carefully to her instructors.
S   V
	Subject + Verb + Object
	
	The students write paragraphs every week.
	  S V O
	She bought a new car last week.
	S V O
	The teacher gives homework often.
	  S V O

Subject + Linking Verb + Adjective She is happy at her new job. S V adjective He feels comfortable in that class. S V adjective You seem tired today. S V adjective	

**Subject + Linking Verb + Noun
(identification)**
 	
I am a teacher.
S V   noun
My cousin became an engineer after college.
    S   V   noun
Your present is a book.
    S V noun	

**Subject + Linking Verb +
Prepositional Phrase (location)**
 	
Your shoes are in the closet.
      S   V   prepositional phrase
The party was at my house last night.
      S   V   prepositional phrase
The bank is around the corner.
      S V prepositional phrase	

There is/There are + Noun
 	
There is a ring on her finger.
    S   V   noun
There are three rings on her finger.
    S V noun	

Sentence Combining Chart

Coordinating Conjunctions	Subordinating Conjunctions
Position in Sentence **middle** _____ _____ _____ (clause) conjunction (clause)	**Position in Sentence** **middle** _____ _____ _____ (clause) conjunction (clause) **OR** **beginning** _____ _____ _____ conjunction (clause) (clause)
Punctuation **comma** _____ , _____ _____	**Punctuation** **no comma** _____ _____ _____ **OR** **comma** _____ _____ , _____
ADDITION: *and* Joe took a long bike ride yesterday, **and** he rode all over the park.	REASON: *because* Joyce is returning to school **because** she wants a new career. **Because** Joyce wants a new career, she is returning to school.
CONTRAST: *but* Joe took a long bike ride yesterday, **but** he did not get tired at all.	CONDITION: *if* Bill exercises every day **if** he is not too tired. **If** Bill is not too tired, he exercises every day.
RESULT: *so* Joe took a long bike ride yesterday, **so** he was very tired when he returned home.	TIME WORDS: *before / after / until / when / while / as* We always read the book **before** we go to class. **After** I come home, I always do my homework. She works on her homework **until** she finishes it. The telephone rang **while** I was eating my dinner. **When** I heard the telephone, I was eating my dinner. **As** I was eating my dinner, my brother was finishing his homework.
CHOICE: *or* Joe will take a bike ride this afternoon, **or** he will wash the car.	

VOCABULARY INDEX

access, 122, 124
accommodate, 93, 96
advance, 93, 97
agriculture, 62, 65
ancestor, 62, 65
Anglos, 70
announce, 3, 6
anonymous, 151, 153
anthropologist, 34
anthropology, 34
application, 122, 126
attractive, 35, 37
autobiography, 82

barrio, 82
biography, 82
blended, 123
blending, 62, 64
blog, 123
body painting, 35, 39
boycott, 84
broad, 122, 124
burst, 167

career, 93, 96
catching up on, 3, 7
century, 62, 65
challenging, 3, 6
chat room, 122, 126
Chicana, 82
circulate, 151, 153
citizen, 62, 65
claw, 155
clay, 35, 38
colonize, 62, 65
competitive, 93, 97
compressed workweek, 93, 97
conquistador, 62, 65
consist of, 93, 97
contracted specialist, 94, 97
convenience, 122, 125
convenient, 122, 125
cope, 151, 153

core hours, 93, 97
cosmetics, 35, 37
create, 151, 154

deadline, 122, 125
decoration, 35, 39
descend, 62, 65
design, 35, 37
device, 122, 125
discussion board, 122, 126
disk, 35, 39
disruptive, 4, 6
due, 4, 6

entire, 122, 125
evidence, 151
exaggerated, 152, 153
exclusively, 93, 97
expectation, 3, 6

fable, 151
face-to-face, 123, 126
fast, 84
feel free to, 3, 7
fictitious, 151, 153
flexible, 93, 96
folk story, 151
folktale, 151
forum, 122, 126
freelance, 94, 97

generation, 35, 38
globalization, 93, 96
goals, 3, 6
guideline, 3, 6

hand in, 3, 7
hero, 151, 154
humorous, 152, 154
hunger strike, 84
hybrid, 123

immigrant, 62, 65
impose, 62, 64

independently, 123, 125
inhabitant, 62, 65
insert, 35, 38
interactive, 93, 97
is responsible for, 3, 7

journey, 62, 64

legend, 151
livestock, 62, 65
lumber, 62, 65

mine, 62, 65
moral, 151, 153
mummies, 35, 38
myth, 151

natural materials, 35, 39
nomadic people, 40
non-degree, 122, 125

objective, 3, 6
occurrence, 151, 154
online, 122, 126
on time, 3, 7
option, 93, 96
oral, 151, 154
origin, 151, 154

pay attention, 4, 7
permanent, 35, 38
piercing, 35, 39
plot, 152, 154
post, 122, 125
productive, 93, 96
professional, 93, 97

railroad, 62, 65
real time, 122, 126
rebel, 62, 64
recreation, 122, 126
remaining, 123, 126
remote, 151, 154
removable, 35, 38
resemble, 151, 154

resource, 122, 126
ritual, 35, 37

settler, 62, 65
sharp, 35, 38
staggered, 93, 97
stretch, 35, 37
strike, 80
successful, 3, 6
survive, 151, 154
syllabus, 3, 5

take advantage of, 3, 7
tale, 151, 154
tattooing, 35, 39

telecommuting, 93, 97
temporary, 35, 39
territory, 62
thrilling, 151, 155
tip, 3, 5
tool, 122, 126
torch, 155
traditional, 35, 37
treaty, 62, 64

unappealing, 35, 38
underwent/undergo, 62, 65
undocumented, 75

various, 35, 38
version, 151, 155
virtually, 93, 97

wages, 62, 64
whirling, 155

SKILLS INDEX

a/an/the, in titles, 14
Additional information, introductory
  transitions showing, 99
Adjectives, 46, 47
  linking verbs with, 40–41, 42–44
after, 157, 158, 208. *See also* Subordinating
  conjunctions
also, 99
and, 67, 69, 208. *See also* Coordinating
  conjunctions
Articles, 14
as, 157, 208
as a result, 100
be, as linking verb, 41
because, 128–138, 208
before, 157, 158, 208. *See also*
  Subordinating conjunctions
Biography, 82–89
Body of essay, 181
Body paragraphs, 181
but, 68, 208. *See also* Coordinating
  conjunctions
Capitalization
  with coordinating conjunctions, 68
  correcting errors with, 105
  of sentences, 9
  with subordinating conjunctions, 129,
    157
  in titles, 14
Checking your work, 26, 29, 56, 87–88,
  116, 146–147, 174–175
Chronological organization
  for instructions/procedures, 107–108
  for narration, 168–171
Classroom procedures, 2
Clauses, 67, 70
  dependent, 130, 157
  independent, 128, 130, 157
Commas, 68, 69, 129, 138, 156–157, 208
Comma splices
  with coordinating conjunctions, 69–70,
    74
  with subordinating conjunctions, 131,
    137–138
  with subordinating conjunctions of time,
    158, 165–166
  with transitions, 101, 105
Compositions. *See* Essays
Compound subjects, 10
Concluding sentences, 16, 77–81, 84,
  108–110, 142–143, 168–170, 178,
  181–182

  in writing process, 87, 116, 145, 173
Conclusion, of essay, 182
Conjunctions
  coordinating, 67–69, 70–73, 161–162,
    208
  subordinating. *See* Subordinating
    conjunctions
Connectors, 67
  coordinating conjunctions as, 67–69,
    70–73
Context clues, to vocabulary, 38–39
Contrast, introductory transitions showing,
  100
Controlling ideas, 17–22, 28, 55, 86
Coordinating conjunctions, 67–69, 70–73,
  161–162, 208
Dependent clauses, combining with
  independent clauses, 130, 157
Description, paragraph organization for,
  46–52
Details, 4–5, 36–37, 63–64, 79, 94, 123,
  152–153, 169, 170. *See also* Supporting
  sentences
Discussion, questions for, 7, 12, 25–26, 34,
  39, 45, 52, 60, 66, 75, 84, 92, 97–98,
  105, 113, 126, 138, 143, 155, 166, 171
Double spacing, 15
Editing, 26, 30, 57, 89, 117, 147, 175
End punctuation, 9, 15
Essays
  body of, 181
  definition of, 178
  expanding paragraphs into,
    179–187
  parts of, 180–182
  similarities and differences between
    paragraphs and, 183
Examples
  introductory transitions showing, 99
  for support, 22–25
Exclamation points, 9, 15
Facts
  opinions versus, 140
  in supporting sentences, 77, 79
Feedback
  about first draft, 26, 30, 56, 89, 116,
    147, 175
  about ideas, 26, 28, 55, 87, 115, 145,
    173, 190–206
First draft
  feedback about, 26, 30, 56, 89, 116,
    147, 175

writing, 26, 28–29, 55, 87, 115, 146,
173–174
for example, 99
for instance, 99
for one thing, 99
Fragments. *See* Sentence fragments
Freewriting, 3, 34, 61, 92, 121, 150
furthermore, 99
however, 100
Ideas
controlling, 17–22, 28, 55, 86
feedback about, 26, 28, 55, 87, 115,
145, 173, 190–206
generation of, 26, 27, 53–54, 85–86,
113–114, 144–145, 172
organizing, 26, 28, 55, 86–87, 114–115,
145, 173
if, 128–138, 208
in addition, 99
in brief, 109
Indenting paragraphs, 14
Independent clauses, 128
combining with dependent clauses, 130,
157
in other words, 100
in short, 109
Instructions, chronological organization for,
107–108
Instructor roles and responsibilities, 2
in sum, 109
in summary, 109
Introduction to essay, 181
Introductory transitions, 99–105
showing examples, 99
Journal writing, 188
Justification, 14
Linking transitions, 101n
Linking verbs, with adjectives, prepositions,
and nouns, 40–44
Lists, punctuation of, 69
Main ideas, 4–5, 36, 63, 94, 123, 152
restating in concluding sentence, 77–78
Maps, 60–61
Margins, 14
Narration, chronological organization for,
168–171
Nouns, 46, 47
linking verbs with, 40–44
lists of, 69
Objects, in sentences, 9–10, 11, 207
on the other hand, 100
Opinions, giving, 140–143
Opposite, introductory transitions showing,
100

or, 68, 69, 208. *See also* Coordinating
conjunctions
Organization
of paragraphs. *See* Paragraph
organization
of thoughts and ideas, 26, 28, 55,
86–87, 114–115, 145, 173
Paragraph organization
for biography, 82–89
chronological, in
instructions/procedures, 107–108
chronological, in narration, 168–171
for description, 46–52
facts and concluding sentences and,
77–81
for giving opinions and providing
reasons, 140–143
supporting sentences and, 16, 17
topic sentences and, 16, 17–22, 23–25
Paragraphs
body, 181
definition of, 13
expanding into essays, 179–187
format of, 13–16, 45–46, 76–77,
106–107, 139, 167
number of sentences in, 16
parts of, 178, 180, 181
sentences in, 15, 16. *See also*
Concluding sentences; Sentences;
Supporting sentences; Topic sentences
similarities and differences between
essays and, 183
title of, 14, 48
transitions in, 22–24
Past progressive verbs, 157
Peer review, 190–206
Periods, 9, 15
Prepositional phrases, 41, 46, 47
Prepositions, 46, 47
linking verbs with, 40–41,
42–44
in titles, 14
Procedures, chronological organization for,
107–108
Process writing. *See* Writing process
Punctuation
commas as, 68, 69, 129, 138, 156–157,
208
with coordinating conjunctions, 68, 208
end, 9, 15
of lists, 69
with subordinating conjunctions, 129,
156–157, 208
Question marks, 9, 15

Questionnaire, 120–121

Quickwriting, 3, 34, 61, 92, 121, 150

Readings

The Beginning of Earth and People, 155

Body Art and Decoration, 35

The Bracero Program, 76

Cesar Chavez, 84

The Changing Workplace, 93–94

Choosing and Scheduling
Classes, 8

Distance Education/Learning, 122–123

Distance Learning: An Excellent
Educational Experience, 139

Dolores Huerta, 82

Early History of Mexican Americans, 62

Finding a Good Place to Study, 20–21

The Fox and the Grapes, 165

Getting Support in Your Classes, 21–22

Henna and Bridal Celebrations, 45

How the World Burst from an Egg, 167

How to Be a Student in a U.S.
Classroom, 3–4

Job Applications, 98

Job Interviews, 106

Migration North, 66

The Milkmaid and Her Pail, 162

The 1920s and 1930s, 75

No Laptops in the Classroom, 142

Pandora's Box, 159

Pecos Bill and the Tornado, 163

Preparing for Classes, 14

Reasons for Body Art/Decoration, 39–40

Replacing a Printer Ink Cartridge, 110

Scheduling Guidelines, 12

Support Across the Campus, 23–24

Susan's Test-Taking Tips, 21

Technology in the Classroom, 127

A Thousand and One Nights, 160

Tips for Taking Online Classes, 138

Traditional Storytelling, 151–152

Twentieth Century Movements Toward
reform, 80

The Wodaabe Geerewol Ceremony, 51

The Woman Who Fell from the Sky, 169

Reasons, providing, 140–143

Restatement, introductory transitions
showing, 100

Result, introductory transitions showing,
100

Review, introductory transitions showing,
100

Run-on sentences

with coordinating conjunctions, 69, 70,
73

with subordinating conjunctions, 131,
136–137, 138

with subordinating conjunctions of time,
158, 163–164

with transitions, 101, 105

Sentence combining, 9

with coordinating conjunctions, 67–69,
70–73, 208

with subordinating conjunctions,
128–138, 208

with subordinating conjunctions of time,
156–166, 208

Sentence fragments, 10–12, 42, 44

with subordinating conjunctions,
130–131, 135–136, 138

with subordinating conjunctions of time,
158, 165

with transitions, 100, 105

Sentences

basic patterns for, 8–12

capitalization of. *See* Capitalization

command or imperative verb forms of,
10n

concluding. *See* Concluding sentences

descriptive, 47–52

introductory transitions in, 99–105

linking verbs with adjectives,
prepositions, and nouns in, 40–44

number in paragraph, 16

in paragraphs, 15, 16

punctuation of. *See* Punctuation

run-on. *See* Run-on sentences

simple, 9, 67

subject, verb, and object pattern of,
9–10, 44, 207

subject and verb pattern of, 8–10, 207

subjects of, 8–12, 67, 207

with subordinating conjunctions of time,
162–163, 168

supporting. *See* Supporting sentences

there as subject of, 42–44

topic. *See* Topic sentences

verbs in, 8–9, 10, 11, 12, 207

word order in. *See* Word order

Simple sentences, 9, 67

so, 68, 208. *See also* Coordinating
conjunctions

Spacing, of paragraphs, 14–15

Stories, 150

Student roles and responsibilities, 2

Subjects of sentences, 8–9, 10, 11, 12, 67,
207

compound, 10

missing. *See* Sentence fragments

Subordinating conjunctions, 128–138, 208
    of time, 156–166, 168, 208
such as, 100
Supporting details
    descriptive, 48–52
    examples for, 22–25
Supporting sentences, 16, 17, 46, 83,
    108–110, 168, 173, 178
    examples in, 22–25
    facts in, 77, 79
    giving opinions and providing reasons
      and, 140–143
    writing, 55
    in writing process, 28, 55, 86, 115, 145,
      173
there, as subject of sentence, 42–44
therefore, 100
Thesis statement, 181
Thoughts, organizing, 26, 28, 55, 86–87,
    114–115, 145, 173
thus, 100
Time, subordinating conjunctions of,
    156–166, 168, 208
Timed writing, 189
Titles, 14, 48
Topics, in topic sentences, 17, 18–19,
    23–25
Topic sentences, 16–25, 46, 48–52, 79–80,
    108–110, 142, 143, 167, 169–170, 173,
    178, 180–181
    format of, 48
    parts of, 17–22, 48
    restating in concluding sentence, 77–78
    writing, 19–22, 55
    in writing process, 28, 55, 86, 114, 145,
      173
Transitions, 22–24
    introductory, 99–105
    linking, 101n
until, 157, 208
Verbs, 67
    linking, 40–44
    past progressive, 157
Verbs in sentences, 8–12, 207
    missing. *See* Sentence fragments

Vocabulary
    idioms, 6–7
    synonyms/definitions, 5–6, 7, 37–38,
      64–65, 95–97, 124–126, 153–155
when, 157, 208
while, 157, 208
Word order, 10, 12, 43–44
    with coordinating conjunctions, 68, 208
    with subordinating conjunctions,
      128–129, 156–157, 208
Writing, 7, 12, 25–26
    of biography, 85
    of descriptive sentences, 47
    in journals, 188
    organizing thoughts for, 31, 58, 90,
      118, 148, 176
    of paragraphs, 110–112
    process of. *See* Writing process
    questions for, 7, 12, 25–26, 39, 45, 52,
      66, 75, 84, 97–98, 105, 113, 126, 138,
      143, 155, 166, 171
    of support sentences, 55
    timed, 189
    topic selection for, 26, 52–53, 85, 113,
      143–144, 171
    of topic sentences, 19–22, 55
Writing process, 26–30, 189
    checking your work and, 26, 29, 56,
      87–88, 116, 146–147, 174–175
    editing step in, 26, 30, 57, 89, 117,
      147, 175
    feedback about first draft step in, 26,
      30, 56, 89, 116, 147, 175
    feedback about ideas step in, 26, 28, 55,
      87, 115, 145, 173, 190–206
    final draft step in, 26, 30, 57, 89, 117,
      147, 175
    first (rough) draft step in, 26, 28–29, 55,
      87, 115, 146, 173–174
    idea generation step in, 26–27, 53–54,
      85–86, 113–114, 144–145, 172
    organizing thoughts and ideas step in,
      26, 28, 55, 86–87, 114–115, 145, 173

Photo Credits

Unit 1
Page 1: Top Left: © Blend Images/Alamy; Bottom Left: © Photos.com/RF; Right: © Peter Glass/Alamy; Page 4: © IndexOpen/RF; Page 8: © Photos.com/RF; Page 20: © Color Day Production/Stone/Getty Images; Page 22: © Richard Elliott/Photographer's Choice/Getty Images; Page 23: © Jack Hollingsworth/Photodisc/Getty Images

Unit 2
Page 33: © Hill Street Studios/Blend Images/Getty Images; Page 34: Top Left: © Wilfried Krecichwost/The Image Bank/Getty Images; Top Right: © Nikreates/Alamy; Center Left: © Ken Straiton/First Light; Center Right: © Frank Barratt/Hulton Archive/Getty Images; Bottom Left: © Danita Delimont/Alamy; Bottom Right: © Radius Images/Jupiterimages; Page 35: Top: © travelstock44/Alamy; 2nd from top: © Fabby Nielsen/Robert Estall photo agency/Alamy; 3rd from top: © Shuji Kobayashi/Stone/Getty Images; Bottom: © Yellow Dog Productions/Stone/Getty Images; Page 40: © Melba Photo Agency/Alamy; Page 45: © Colin Anderson/Blend Images/Alamy; Page 47: © Edward S. Curtis Collection/Library of Congress; Page 50: © Ricardo Beliel/BrazilPhotos/Alamy; Page 51: © Carol Beckwith/Angela Fisher/The Image Bank/Getty Images

Unit 3
Page 59: Top Left: © Lewis Wickes Hine/Library of Congress; Bottom Left: © David R. Frazier Photolibrary, Inc./Alamy; Top Right: © A. Ramey/PhotoEdit, Inc.; Bottom Right: © Jeff Greenberg/PhotoEdit, Inc.; Page 62: © Jacques Jangoux/Alamy; Page 71: © Mark Richards/PhotoEdit, Inc.; Page 74: © George Gardner/The Image Works; Page 76: © AP Images; Page 80: © Bonnie Kamin/PhotoEdit Inc.; Page 82: © Michael Smith/Getty Images; Page 83: © Hector Guerrero/AFP/Getty Images; Page 84: © Jason Laure/The Image Works

Unit 4
Page 91: Top Left: © Photos.com/RF; Top Right: © IndexOpen/RF; Bottom Left: © Digital Vision/Getty Images; Bottom Right: © Yann Layma/The Image Bank/Getty Images; Page 92: Left: © Photos.com/RF; Center: © Baerbel Schmidt/Stone/Getty Images; Right: © Photos.com/RF; Page 93: Top: © IndexOpen/RF; Bottom: © IndexOpen/RF; Page 106: © Photos.com/RF; Page 108: © John Lund/Drew Kelly/Blend Images/Getty Images; Page 110: © geldi/Alamy

Unit 5
Page 119: Top Left: © Paul Vozdic/The Image Bank/Getty Images; Bottom: © Tim Platt/Iconica/Getty Images; Top Right: © IndexOpen/RF; Page 122: Top: © blue jean images; Bottom: © Steve McAlister Productions/The Image Bank/Getty Images; Page 127: © George Doyle/Stockbyte/Getty Images; Page 134: © Kevin Cooley/Taxi/Getty Images; Page 139: © Jupiterimages/Comstock Images/Alamy; Page 142: © George Doyle/Stockbyte/Getty Images

Unit 6
Page 149: Top Left: © Gail Ward/Alamy; Top Right: © Gary Cook/Alamy; Bottom Left: © David Deas/DK Stock/Getty Images; Page 151: Top: © F.J. Bertuch/Superstock, Inc.; Bottom: © Alexandre Laborde/Bibliothèque des Arts Décoratifs Paris/Dagli Orti/The Art Archive; Page 155: © Neue Galerie, Kassel, Germany/© Museumslandschaft Hessen Kassel/Ute Brunzel/The Bridgeman Art Library; Page 159: © Lady Lever Art Gallery, National Museums Liverpool/The Bridgeman Art Library; Page 160: © Private Collection/Photo © Bonhams, London, UK/The Bridgeman Art Library; Page 162: © Mary Evans Picture Library/The Image Works; Page 164: © Bibliotheque Nationale, Paris, France/Lauros/Giraudon/The Bridgeman Art Library; Page 165: Top: © Bibliotheque Nationale, Paris, France/Lauros /Giraudon/The Bridgeman Art Library; Bottom: © Visions of America, LLC/Alamy